365
BOREDOM BUSTING
ACTIVITIES

Fun activities to keep you busy for hours!

Om KIDZ | Om Books International

First Published in 2018

Corporate & Editorial Office
A-12, Sector 64, Noida 201 301,
Uttar Pradesh, India
Phone: +91 120 477 4100
Email: editorial@ombooks.com,
Website: www.ombooksinternational.com

Sales Office
107, Ansari Road, Darya Ganj,
New Delhi 110 002, India
Phone: +91 11 4000 9000
Email: sales@ombooks.com
Website: www.ombooks.com

365

BOREDOM BUSTING
ACTIVITIES

Fun activities to keep you busy for hours!

Om
KIDZ
An imprint of Om Books International

CONTENTS

MARVELLOUS MAY!

JOYOUS JUNE!

JOVIAL JULY!

1. Miswimgn

2. Utiagr

3. Acheb

4. Ripotdar

5. Ncicpi

6. Wokeginma

AWESOME AUGUST!

SWEET SEPTEMBER!

OPTIMISTIC OCTOBER!

NICE NOVEMBER!

DREAMY DECEMBER!

Levels of Difficulty

The activities are categorised into three levels of difficulty. They are Easy, Normal and Challenging.

These are indicated by grey beads in the abacus icon along each activity.

EASY   NORMAL   CHALLENGING

1 Flower power

Solve the crossword to discover the common flowers you can find in a garden.

Across

1. Add a four wheeled vehicle to the word 'nations'. (Plural)
2. A flower that begins with 'OR'. (Plural)
3. A flower which has a 'lip' in its name. (Singular)
4. Donald and ____y Duck. (Singular)
5. Add the opposite of 'a little' to the word 'us'. (Singular)

Down

1. _____ are red, violets are blue. (Plural)
2. Replace a vowel in the word 'puppies'. (Plural)
3. _____ need lots of sunshine to grow. (Plural)

11

365 Boredom Busting Activities

2 Talent in the jungle

It's talent day in the jungle. The badger, deer and eagle are performing for the others. Can you find 10 differences in the pictures?

12

3 Ice cream maze 🍦

I scream! You scream! Everybody screams for an ice cream! Eat your ice cream the right way before it melts!

Start

Finish

 4 Fun on the ferris wheel 🍦

Make words with three letters or more. Create as many as you can. Remember to use the letter in the middle in all the words. Try and make one word using all the letters.

_____

_____

_____

_____

_____

_____

5 Pen holders from toilet paper rolls

The cardboard tubes inside a toilet paper roll can come in very handy. Learn how to make a pen holder.

Materials required: 1 toilet paper tube, glue, acrylic paints, pencil, brushes, cardboard paper and wrapping paper

Steps:
1. Cut a circular piece from the cardboard. Stick it at the bottom end of the roll to close it.
2. Decorate it with wrapping paper or paint it.
3. If you choose to paint, first draw anything you like, then colour it. Let it dry overnight.
4. Decorate your pen holder in bright colours. Acrylic paints are the best.

Once dry, your pen holder is ready for use!

6 Word play

A word has been spelled out using pictures. Can you guess what the word is?

FRIS +   = _____

(Hint: A game you play outdoors)

 + +  =

_____

(Hint: You play this game with a shuttlecock)

7 # Family portrait

Draw pictures of your parents, brother or sister and yourself in each frame. Below each of the doodles, write their names and yours.

 8 # Lost at sea

A ship capsized in a storm at sea. A survivor held on to a log and managed to reach a deserted island. Tired and confused he found this message written in the sand. Help him decipher the message!

eelcomw ot ruo lsidan. ew lliw
eb ckab thiw thesloc dan doof.
reaf ton. uoy rea fase.

9 Farm fresh

Ever spent time on a farm? Solve this crossword puzzle to see what you remember of your visit.

Across:
1. The fields are full of this
4. A huge dear like animal with antlers
5. The farmers _____ the field
8. Old MacDonald had a ____
9. Opposite of stand
10. Something used to carry objects
12. An animal that pulls carriages
14. A female gander is called this

Down:
1. A young male horse
2. The young one of a dog
3. An animal that gives milk
6. The young one of a sheep
7. Animals that chase mice
8. A kind of evergreen tree
9. Do re mi fa __ la ti do
11. Animal whose young one is called kid
12. "Don't _ _ _ all the ice cream"
13. You see with your ___

10 Who ate the food?

Button, the tabby cat, had to share his bed and dish with Phyllis and Ryan, the bobtail cats.

1. If Button ate oats, then Phyllis ate that too.
2. If Phyllis drank milk, Ryan would not eat what Button ate.
3. If Ryan ate fish and Phyllis drank milk, who always ate from the same dish? _____

_____

11 Wonderland

Replace or remove some of the letters to finally reach a single letter. Remember to change one letter at a time and use 'W' in all the words.

12 Pirate the parrot ⌇⌇⌇

Give Pirate his eye, scarf, pirate hat and a
scenery that would suit his personality.

13 Crazy about cars ⌇⌇⌇

In the grid below, can you find the names of the different parts of a car?

The list of the parts of cars:

1. Engine
2. Exhaust
3. Petrol
4. Seat
5. Belt
6. Keys
7. Gears
8. Boot
9. Mirror
10. Sunroof
11. Wheel
12. Pedal
13. Headlights
14. Radio
15. Windscreen
16. Bonnet
17. Bumper
18. Axle

```
E H S J S B D B J V Y S E P U
J X P F K R H J P E N G I N E
G P H M B A S I E C X A Z J Q
E E R A V K X M T F F M S N M
A D A N U E E R R O Y H E H U
R A D X I S E W O E E E A M C
S L I V H P T R L V R A T C K
L A O L M O N X R C V D B C K
O X X U O U A I S V R L E B E
V P B B S I J D B B N I L W Y
S B O V E T N T O Y P G T H S
J T N D W I U M N K T H R E V
L V Y D W M N Q N X J T N E H
M I R R O R Z B E L R S M L K
M E P D E K W S T F Z Q C C N
```

14 Dream doodle

Imagine you dreamt of a candy land where everything was made of candy. Draw your dream.

15 Nomnom spaghetti maze

Can you find the strands of spaghetti that join together? Write the numbers in the box provided.

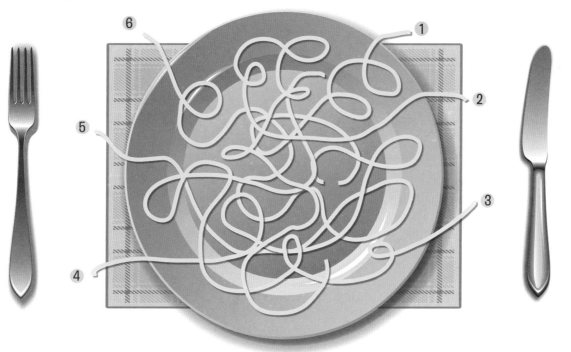

16 Two ninjas

Can you imitate these two ninja moves?

Materials required: Craft paper, a pair of scissors, scale/ruler and pencil

Method:

1. Get two square pieces of paper
2. Use a tracing paper to mark out the shapes and cut accordingly.
3. Use the cut out shapes to make the two ninjas.

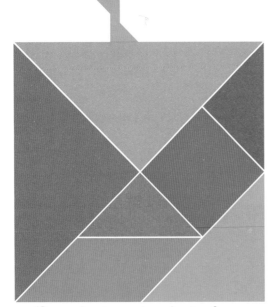

*Remember to use two sheets of craft paper to make the two ninjas because one sheet will be enough for just one.

17 Star of wonder

Can you tell how many triangles there are in this image? What is the other image you see in it?

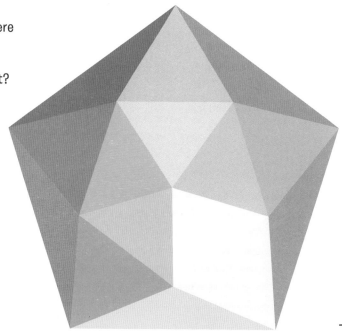

_____

18 Guess the number

Can you guess the answers to the number problems given below? Here's a clue: Both the sums have the same answer.

4 x 21 = 42 x 2 =   _____

9 x 10 = 18 x 5 =   _____

45 + 45 + 180 = 180 + 45 + 45 =   _____

8 + 10 + 2016 = 1017 x 2 =   _____

19 ⭐ Under the sea ‡‡‡

Colour the animals that live under the sea. Use the colour code given below.

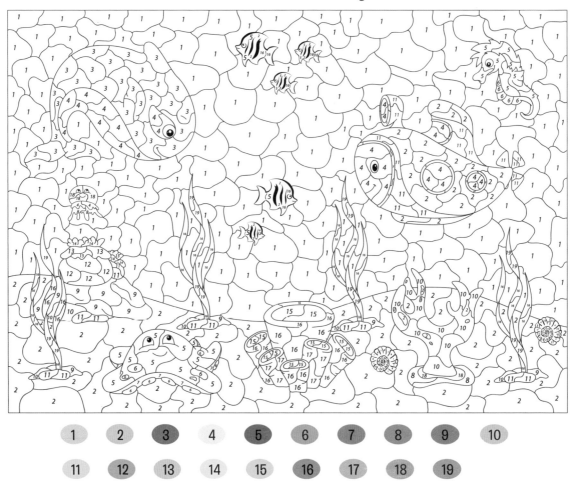

| 1 | 2 | 3 | 4 | 5 | 6 | 7 | 8 | 9 | 10 |

| 11 | 12 | 13 | 14 | 15 | 16 | 17 | 18 | 19 |

20 ⭐ The mad hatter ‡‡‡

Let us get crafty and make some paper hats!

A fairly easy method and the best part is, you only need craft paper. So, let's not wait any longer and get started!

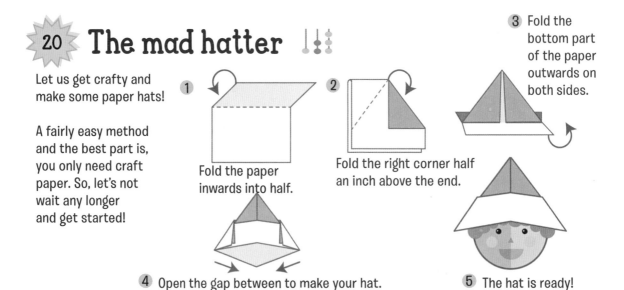

1. Fold the paper inwards into half.

2. Fold the right corner half an inch above the end.

3. Fold the bottom part of the paper outwards on both sides.

4. Open the gap between to make your hat.

5. The hat is ready!

21 Pick the profession

Solve the crossword below and discover the different jobs people do.

Across:
1. A _____ puts out fire
2. _____ is a surgery specialist
3. They teach children
4. Helps run the school
5. Plays a character in a movie
6. They create and animate cartoons

Down:
1. He takes care of our health
2. A _____ writes books
3. An _____ fixes electrical problems
4. A _____ practices the law
5. Cakes, cupcakes and pastries are made by them

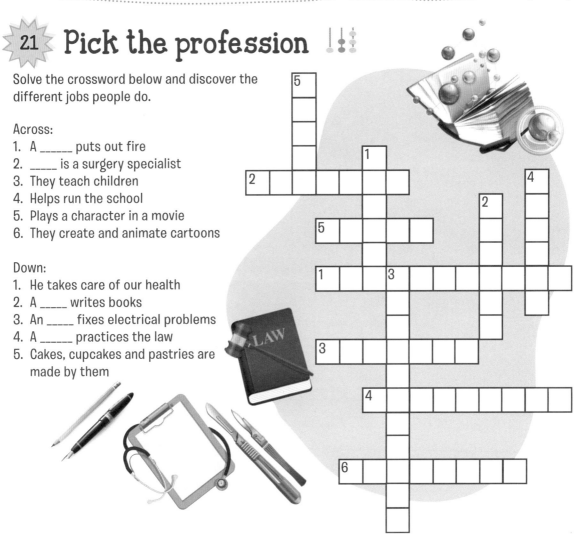

22 Super shapes

Draw the missing shape in the boxes provided to complete the pattern.

23 Which way is the design moving?

Look at the illusion for a few minutes to see the effect, then write down in which way it appears to be moving.

_____

24 The native warrior

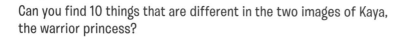

Can you find 10 things that are different in the two images of Kaya, the warrior princess?

25 Sea creatures

Draw a beautiful picture with sea creatures in it.

26 The mole and his carrot

Fred, the mole, has stolen a carrot from the garden. Help him find his way home without getting caught.

27 Day at the beach

It's a lovely day to be at the beach! Look for the words written in the list in the grid below.

1. Towel
2. Sunscreen
3. Frisbee
4. Stereo
5. Shades
6. Umbrella
7. Mat
8. Bag
9. Hat
10. Food
11. Drinks
12. Flipflops

```
H M A D R I N K S E W P M U J
E R M B O U M P R W Z C N M J
X K N P H P S E L G V D Y B H
B M T B D R S P Y F W P L R P
H A T D B S U X C S T E R E O
I B M A T X N G E X M P Q L C
B Y Z Y M F S V W W S T R L C
S T U K R L C W A F P F L A D
E X E D R I R H B Y A R X Y I
H L O E P P E L C L U I W T H
M V K T G F E H B A G S H T J
K F D C A L N B N K J B I P F
G V O L K O Q K T O W E L V V
V N F O Z P C N C D A E U F Y
S W I W D S H A D E S U L G E
```

28 Blooming pots!

Roses are red, Violets are blue.
Complete the picture and doodle it too!

29 The hand animals

Use light to create some fun shadow paintings!

Materials required: Pencil, book, eraser, paints or sketches, table lamp

Method:

1. Place a table lamp in front of the book. You should be able to see shadows over the empty space. Adjust according to where you want to make your shadow painting.
2. Get your parent, sibling or friend to make a hand gesture to form the shadow of an animal on the page.
3. Draw an outline of the shadow that is cast on your page using a pencil. Ask them to remove their hands and continue painting.
4. Keep the shadow black or grey in colour but add a colourful background.
5. You can try making a bird, or rabbit or even a dog!

30 Poodle doodle ⋮⋮⋮

Give Poo the poodle, a kennel that you can doodle.

31 Odd socks ⋮⋮⋮

A man has 53 socks in his drawer: 21 identical red, 15 identical blue and 17 identical black. The room is completely dark. How many socks must he take out from his collection to make 100 percent certain he has a pair of red socks?

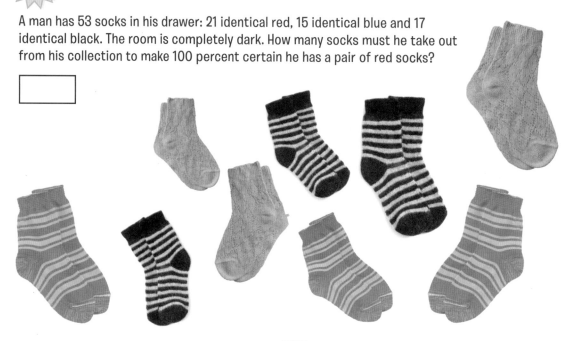

32 A space race

Fun
FEBRUARY!

Add, replace or remove one letter or more to complete
this space mission.

	Hint: Another word for competition.
	Hint: A detective can ___ your whereabouts.
	Hint: Another word for poise or charm.
	Hint: A delicate fabric made with thread or yarn.
	Hint: A metal weapon.
	Hint: One in a game of cards is called ____.
	Hint: Drop the 's' from the word below to increase your ___ ace.
	HINT: Outer sp_c_e.

33 The man at St. Ives

Read the paragraph below and answer the question.

As I was going to St. Ives
I met a man with seven wives.
Each wife had seven sacks,
Each sack had seven cats,
Each cat had seven kits;
Kits, cats, sacks and wives,

How many were going to St. Ives?

_____

34 Geometric patterns

Find the missing piece by looking at the options below.

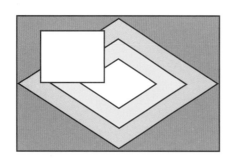

A   B   C   D

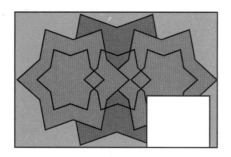

A   B   C   D

35 Home sweet home ♩♪♪

Look for words that are related to a home in this word search.

```
A L I V I N G R O O M A K B U
J T V N D A U P B F V I M E A
B R T Q E T P L A Z T A N D W
Y E F I O I I M W C O T L R I
P E I T C C Q U H M E R H O P
B V T E X D S E L R I F U O E
L T W D J H N Y T O J O A M X
P R R W K G Q A K N U W L R J
G F H O P Z I F I P A D T D Q
A Z H W B N G N B E L C Z W V
R Y L I M O D I B T R P Y N H
A O L N B A L C O N Y S B V G
G H N D G E U T P O O D E C F
E T I O V R R O F A M I L Y A
I J V W A S H R O O M G N U I
```

List of words:
1. Family
2. Garage
3. Kitchen
4. Bedroom
5. Livingroom
6. Attic
7. Cot
8. Window
9. Washroom
10. Balcony

36 Adventures outside ♩♪♪

Let's have some fun with adventure sports themed flash cards!
Materials required: 2.5 x 3.5 cms rectangular card paper sheets (10 nos), sketch pens, glue, images representing the action words

Method:
1. On one side of the cards, write down the names of different adventure sports around the world. Examples: Parkour, skate boarding, sky diving etc.
2. On the other side, paste or draw images that represent the sports.
3. Once done, shuffle the cards up and play with a friend.

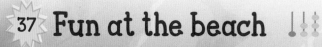

37 Fun at the beach

Alice and Ron can't wait to go on their boat. Help them get there from the shore!

Finish

Start

38 Sails ahoy!

Aye aye, Cap'n!
Let the sailor within you float away by drawing a ship or a sailboat!

Mrs G's baking session

Mrs G's baking classes are a huge hit! Let's see how many differences you can find in the images below.

 ## Guess the idioms

Can you look at the clues below and tell what the idioms are?

  = _____ spilled milk

 = _____ of _____

   = _____ of the _____

41 Let's go to the zoo

The zoo is a fascinating place to visit. Let's see if you recognise these zoo animals. Look at the pictures of the animals and solve the crossword puzzle.

Home is where the heart is

This house seems to be missing some of its parts! Why don't you draw the rest of it?

43 Cats versus dogs

Look at the image for a minute. Which animals can you see in it?

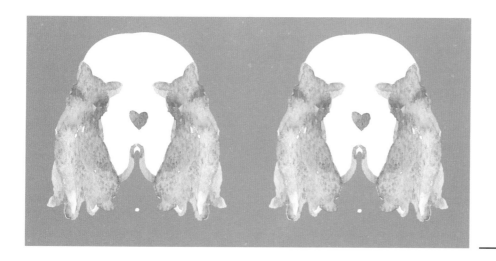

44 Unscramble the ones with the guts!!!!

Ms Simone, the English teacher at school, has given you a surprise spelling test. Unfortunately, she has jumbled the words. It's up to you to solve this puzzle and score points. Go ahead, try and unscramble the words!

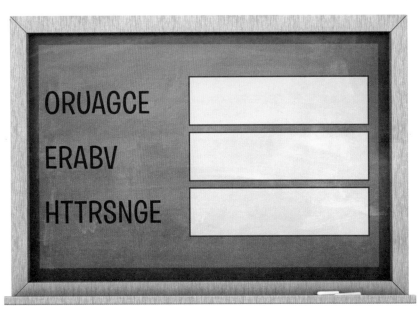

ORUAGCE

ERABV

HTTRSNGE

45 Find the turkey's shadow !!!!

Can you find Uri the turkey's matching shadow?

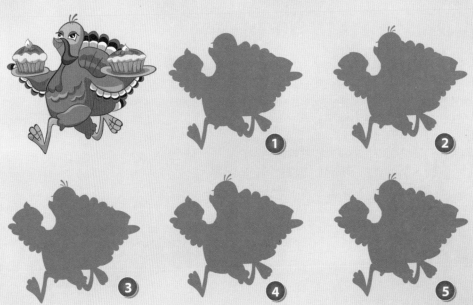

46 Fruity frenzy

How many apples would you have, if you take 3 apples from a group of 5?

_____

47 Fishing games

Two fathers, Ralph and Ronald along with two sons, one named Marc, go fishing. Each of them catches one fish. So why do they bring home only three fish?

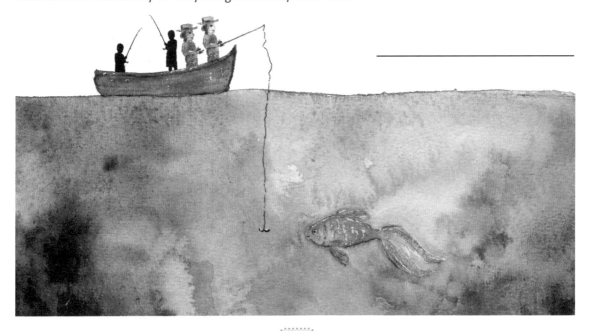

_____

48 Mr Cheesy gets his cheese

Help Mr Cheesy the mouse find the right path to reach his block of cheese.

49 Shroomy the mushroom

Try and copy the same drawing of Shroomy the mushroom. Colour it as you like with spots, lines or even with a butterfly.

50 Heart-shaped butter cookies

Today, let's bake some easy heart-shaped butter cookies!

Materials required: 1 cup butter, 1 cup sugar, 1 egg, 3 cups all-purpose flour, 1/4 teaspoon salt, 2 tsp vanilla extract/essence, heart-shape cookie cutter and cookie sheets (parchment paper)

Method:

1. In a large bowl, mix the butter and sugar until you get a creamy and fluffy mix. Beat in the egg, then add in some vanilla essence. Mix well.
2. Add the flour, salt and stir in the sugar. You should make a thick dough that isn't too hard.
3. Once the dough is ready, cover it with cling wrap and chill for an hour. Meanwhile, chill the cookie sheets and preheat your oven to about 200°C.
4. Take the dough out and roll it with the rolling pin. Use the cutter to make shapes and then place the cookie dough on the sheets.
5. Bake the cookies for 8-10 minutes, till the edges are golden brown. Remove the cookies and leave them to cool.
6. It takes about 1 hour and 45 minutes to get these delicious cookies ready, counting preparation time, chilling the dough and then baking it.
7. Decorate the cookies with icing or castor sugar.

51 Summer time and a picnic ⌵⌵⌵

Draw a fun picnic scene.

52 Foodie's delight ⌵⌵⌵

Add, replace or remove one
letter or more to get to the top.

Hint: ____ and fried

Hint: Speaking with a _____

Hint: A number of collected items

Hint: Fog

Hint: Final

Hint: Another word for history

Hint: Opposite of slow

Hint: Close palm into a ___

Hint: Survives on water

Hint: You put food in this

Dish

53 Same-same but different!

Skrat and his brother Ratty are twins. They both look the same, yet are different. Can you spot the differences between the two?

54 Magic numbers

Replace the number signs with mathematical symbols to make this equation work.

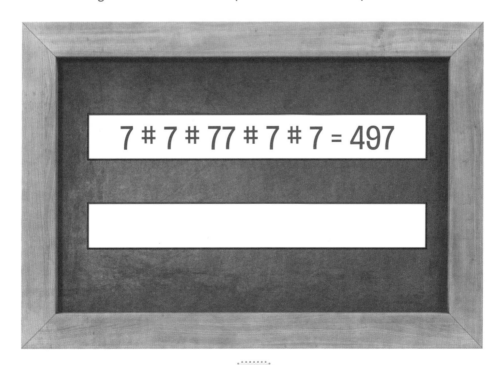

7 # 7 # 77 # 7 # 7 = 497

55 Stairway to Tanville

Make this stairway to enter the whimsical land of Tanville.

Method: Turn the squares on the right into a stairway. Take a square piece of paper and trace the shapes as shown below on the right. Cut them out and figure out how to make the stairway.

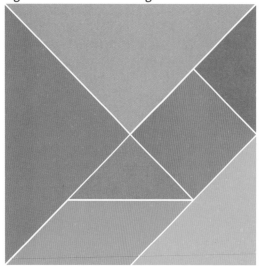

56 School time

Solve this school related word search by circling the words listed below. Be sure to look for hidden words written backwards as well.

```
D R A O B K C A L B T C Y D W
C V Z I V R P R A Y E R C C C
H Y Y D C R T F K E M K L B Z
A Z L I S E K B X D N U O R G
L G M B A V Q G M S A B O V I
K F I C M D N U O R G Y A L P
O J H B H E P S H X U K S M W
R E M Z L W S F X B W B A U M
R Z N N C L A S S M A T E S G
T S C H O O L F A L T E E M G
S R M T E R E T S U D K T U I
Q M E E T I N G C Q W C Y U G
L A P I C N I R P D K I U H B
B F I G D U M U P Q H R N D U
U W M O O R S S A L C C V J S
```

List of words:

1. Classroom
2. Classmates
3. Blackboard
4. Prayer
5. Bus
6. Cricket
7. Playground
8. Meeting
9. Principal
10. Chalk
11. Duster
12. School

57 Off to the circus!

A visit to a circus is aways an unforgettable experience. Even if you haven't visited one, use your imagination to draw a circus over the puzzle layout given here. Take a copy of your drawing and paste it on a sheet of cardboard. Make sure you cut the pieces neatly to create your very own handmade puzzle!

58 The red train

The red train usually goes "Woot woot!" as it drives on. But lately it hasn't been very happy. You see, it is missing a few pieces. Match the circles below to the right parts in the image to complete the happy picture!

59 Food for thought!

Find the correct letter for each clue to spell an eight-letter word that is something yummy to eat.

The first letter is in pear but not in tear. _____

The second letter is in harp but not in hop. _____

The third letter is in horizon but not in horror. _____

The fourth letter is in scene but not in seen. _____

The fifth letter is in pack but not in perk. _____

The sixth letter is in knight but not in night. _____

The seventh letter is in leap but not in loop. _____

The eighth letter is in snack but not in knack. _____ _____

60 Help the tropical fish

Stripy and Flo are trying to get to each other. Help Flo get through the maze and reach her friend.

61 Bookmarks for the bookworms! ⡇⡇⡇

Merry MARCH!

Turn colourful greeting cards into bookmarks! Instead of throwing out old cards, use them to create different things. For example, make a bookmark.

Materials required: Old greeting cards, scissors, a punch machine, a pencil, a ruler, paints and string/wool

Method:

1. Cut a greeting card into the shape you want. Use a ruler to measure how long you want the bookmark to be.
2. For a rectangular one, measure 3 x 6 inches. For a square one, measure 4 x 4 inches.
3. With a pencil, draw an outline on the card. Then cut it out.
4. At the centre of one side of the cardpaper, punch a hole. This is where you will add the string or wool later.
5. Pick the colour of your choice and paint the card.
6. Let it dry for a few hours. Decorate the bookmark by writing your name in big letters or using different colours to paint it.
7. Add a tassel or a few strands of wool tied together and your bookmark is ready!
8. To make it more fun, you can stick on confetti or lace to form a border along the bookmark.

62 The hidden symbol

Look at the image for a few minutes and guess what is hidden.

_____

63 Dizzy digits

Read the puzzle below and guess the answer!

1. What is the 4 digit number in which:
   - the first digit is one-fifth the last
   - the second and third are the last digits multiplied by 3

_____

2. The second hand lies on:
   - the third letter, of this time, is also a math sign
   - the second is an l and the first is the number 7 on a keypad

_____

3. The hour hand lies on:
   - the last day of the month of June

_____

64 Chef Melanie cooks!

Chef Melanie has prepared her favourite pot roast. Someone took a picture of her while she was cooking. But something looks different. Can you tell what the differences in the pictures are?

65 Fun at the circus

Doodle what a day at the circus would be like for you. You can look at different books or photos, or get your friends and family to help you with this activity.

66 Where does the minute hand go?

Look at the clocks and the time they are showing. Can you tell where the minute hand goes for the third clock in the first row and fourth in the second row? If you choose to leave it in the same place, what time would it show?

67 Motion for emotion

Find the different types of emotions hidden in this puzzle.

List of words:

1. Happy
2. Thoughtful
3. Healthy
4. Amused
5. Joyful
6. Confident
7. Proud
8. Sulky
9. Afraid
10. Amazed
11. Delighted
12. Hopeful

```
A X Y P F H J H L I C H H B S
M L P R U F E U A P G T O U U
A S T O R K F A Z P K J P E L
Z J T U H Y U F L Q P T E Z K
E W M D O A U P K T S Y F O Y
D E R J H P S G U E H O U I X
D C L C Z B V Y Z B J Y L R I
L U C A E T K F E B C A H R P
R V W H T H O U G H T F U L D
V H A I O E A X B S O M Y A K
P N Q I Y I D Z C I F U B F C
D C O N F I D E N T I T B R R
R Y Q O O S A M U S E D K A O
F Y L C B T N M F N J T Z I O
D E L I G H T E D Y Y R B D T
```

68 Cricket mania

Draw a batsman holding the bat. Use green and yellow colour to colour the cricket pitch!

69 Add, multiply or divide

Find out what should replace the blank triangles. The first two have been done for you.

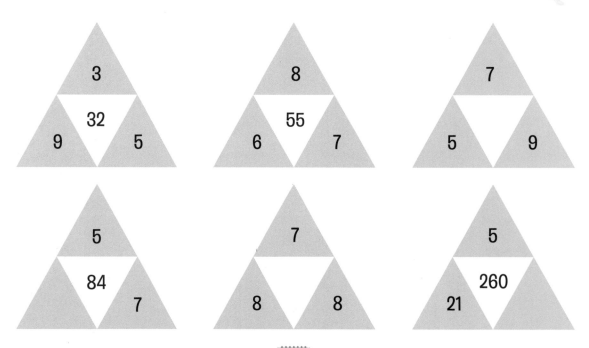

70 Easter eggs feast

This is a fun activity, but you're going to need your parents to help with it!

Materials required: A dozen eggs, food colouring, vinegar, water, a vessel for boiling the eggs, zip lock bags, paper towels and a spoon

Method:
1. Boil the eggs for a few minutes.
2. Take them out and gently crack them all over. Do not peel any as yet.
3. Put the eggs into a zip lock bag. Add some food colouring in too.
4. Refrigerate the eggs for 30 minutes so that they absorb the colour.
5. Rinse the eggs in water to wash off excess colour.
6. Splash on some vinegar so that the colour sticks.
7. Pat the eggs with paper towels till they are dry.

Your marbled Easter eggs are ready!

71 Guess the verbs

Solve the crossword by guessing the right words!

Across:
1. Breaking free
2. Moving your head up and down in either agreement/disagreement
3. Opposite of close
4. When you want to speak to someone you ___ their name

Down:
1. Another word for save
2. To grasp or seize suddenly
3. Quick movement or jump
4. You have to ____ the keys to play a note on the piano

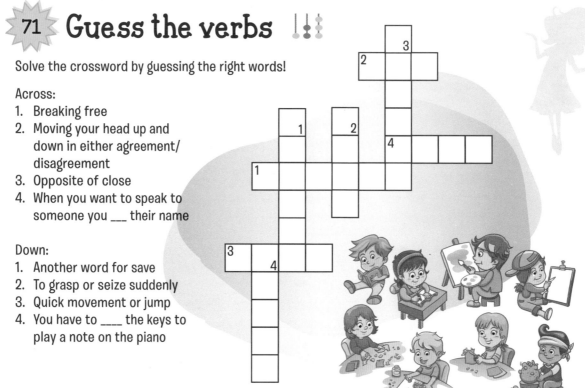

72 Hungry panda

Draw a baby panda sitting next to a bamboo plant and eating it.

73 In the palm of your hand ⁝⁝⁝

Time to make an interesting jigsaw puzzle.
Draw an image of your palm on the puzzle pattern given below. Once that's done, you can make a copy of it and paste it on a card paper or cardboard and cut along the outlines of the pieces and before you know it, your palm puzzle is ready!

74 Let's go for a drive ⁝⁝⁝

Add/Replace or remove one letter or more to go from Car to Drive.

	Hint: Another word for pilot or steer
	Hint: A taxi _____
	Hint: To plunge head first into water
	Hint: Short for David
	Hint: To challenge someone
	Hint: A kind of a rabbit
	Hint: A string instrument
	Hint: Another way of saying pointy
	Hint: To give what you have to others
	Hint: To frighten someone
	Hint: Mark on the skin from a wound
Car	

75 Animal affairs

Four kids went to an unusual pet store. Each one picked a different animal to take home.
Can you match the child with his or her new friend by following the clues given?

	Dragon	Manatee	Sea Serpent	Unicorn
Sergei				
Darius				
Mishka				
Ursla				

1. No child has a pet that starts with the same letter as their name.
2. Darius doesn't have a pet that lives in the water.
3. Mishka is allergic to smoke.
4. Sergei's pet loves to fly.

76 Havoc hotel

Can you answer this question?

13 people went to a hotel that had 12 rooms. Each guest wanted their own room. The bellboy had a solution to this problem. He requested the 13th guest to wait a little, with the first guest, in room number 1. Meaning, there were two people in the first room. He then took the third guest to room number 2, the fourth to number three... and so on till the 12th guest was taken to room number 11. He then returned to room number 1 and took the 13th guest to room number 12, still vacant. Can you tell if everyone gets their own room?

_____

_____

77 Walk in the park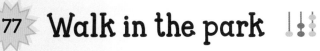

Turn this incomplete image of a park into a beautiful one!

78 Lava in a glass

You've heard of hot lava erupting from the earth's surface but how about cool lava in a glass? Well, let's make some today.

Materials required: A glass of water, 1/4th cup vegetable oil, 1 teaspoon salt, food colouring

Method:
1. Fill 3/4th of the glass with water.
2. Add 5 drops of blue food colouring.
3. Pour the vegetable oil, slowly, into the glass. Notice how it floats up.
4. Sprinkle the salt over the oil, it will create blobs of lava that will float around. (Oil being lighter than water ends up floating. Salt being heavier than oil, sinks down but take some oil with it. Once it dissolves, it floats back up.)
5. Keep adding the salt for the effect to last longer.

79 Mind your math

Find a list of topics that you study under math!

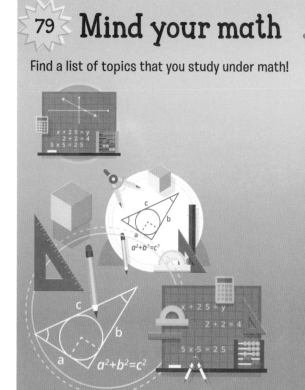

```
O Q T K O K J H E N
O J D E C I M A L S
A L G E B R A W B D
U F R A C T I O N S
W A D D I T I O N M
Y N B V L P I T A X
B L G E O M E T R Y
U B B C S Z A Z A A
P E R C E N T A G E
E D I V I S I O N C
```

List of words: geometry, fractions, decimals, division, tax, algebra, percentage, addition

The glass shoe

Find 10 differences between both the pictures.

 Robot love

Can you tell which hand of the robot is holding out his heart?
Draw a line over the correct hand.

82 Confused Ken

Ken loves solving puzzles. Sadly, he can't figure out this one. Do you think you can help him solve these questions?

Q: What comes twice in a week, once in a year and never in a day?

_____

_____

_____

83 At sea

Below, you will find words spelled out using images. Can you guess what they are?

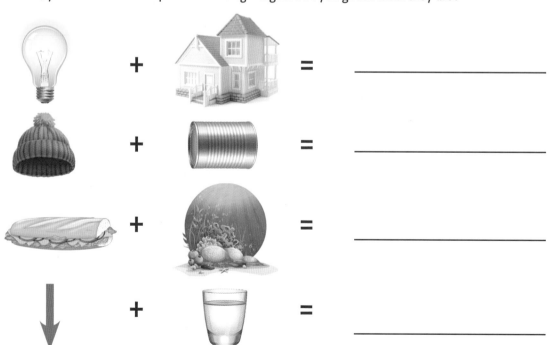

84 Give the dog a bone

Help little Pooch get through this maze to reach his bone.

85 Camel in the desert

Use your imagination and complete the drawing of the camels and their human friends.

86 The vintage collection

Solve this vintage crossword puzzle.

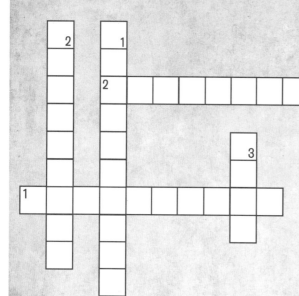

Across:
1. Ladies use this to store their make up when travelling
2. A camera that gives an instant photograph

Down:
1. A device used for typing before keyboards were made
2. Messages sent by a telegraph
3. Service that delivers letters or couriers/parcels

87 Superhero you

Draw yourself as a superhero! Use as many colours as you want and give yourself a superhero name too!

88 Solve the message

Dr Evil has sent his arch nemesis Mr Goodie Two-shoes a coded message regarding the children he holds hostage. Help Mr Goodie Two-shoes decode this message by replacing the numbers with letters on the keypad.

"If you want the children, answer this riddle!" Dr Evil.
9428 4637 ROUND AND 276863
ON A 467732225?

_____

A 22768735.

89 From ice to water

Add, replace or remove one or more letters to go up the word ladder and guess the last word.

Hint: When ice melts, it becomes _____?

Hint: A person who walks dogs is a dog _____?

Hint: To move around using your legs.

Hint: To speak.

Hint: What is the stem of a plant called?

Hint: Use it to write on blackboards.

Hint: A goblet you can drink from.

Hint: Feeling of ill will or anger.

Hint: A girl in Wonderland.

Ice

90 Animals in the jungle

Try and find 10 differences between the two pictures of the jungle.

91 Charming snake

Find the snake's matching shadow.

92 Paper cup shakers

Let's make some cool percussion instruments! You can actually use these as accompaniments, in your school band or even at home when you want to sing.

Materials required: 2 disposable paper cups, a handful of beads preferably of different sizes or uncooked rice, glue or tape, a brush and paints

Method:
1. Place the beads or rice in one cup.
2. Cover it with the empty cup and ensure the wide sides are one over the other.
3. Either use glue or tape to attach both the cups together.
4. Paint or doodle over it to give it a fun appearance.

*Remember to customise the shakers according to how you want it. These make cute gifting items too. So go crazy with decorating them!

93 Conserve the Earth

Can you solve this puzzle which tells you about our planet Earth?

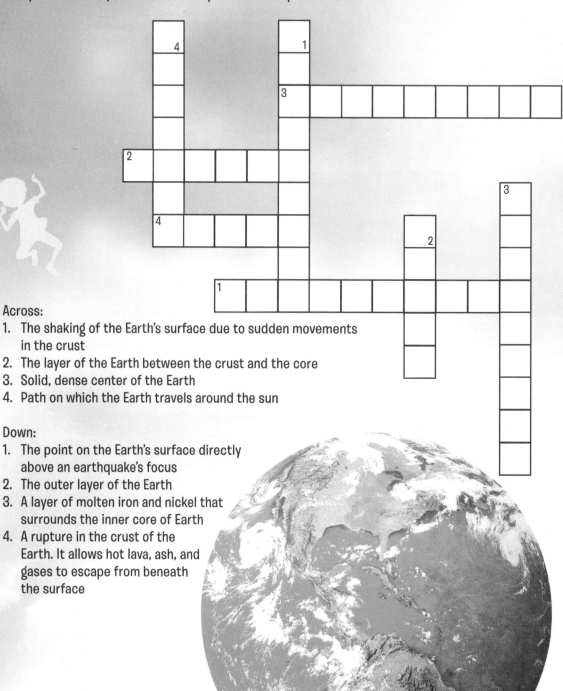

Across:
1. The shaking of the Earth's surface due to sudden movements in the crust
2. The layer of the Earth between the crust and the core
3. Solid, dense center of the Earth
4. Path on which the Earth travels around the sun

Down:
1. The point on the Earth's surface directly above an earthquake's focus
2. The outer layer of the Earth
3. A layer of molten iron and nickel that surrounds the inner core of Earth
4. A rupture in the crust of the Earth. It allows hot lava, ash, and gases to escape from beneath the surface

94 Mosaic monuments

Look at the funky representation of monuments from around the world. Can you tell which monument comes next in this pattern?

95 From a fairytale

Fairytales are about princes, princesses, morals and a lot more. Let's see if you can find some of the words in the grid below.

```
W G N I K S N E R O S W P W Y
Y I G O O D E W G X P S R J W
Y T U A E B E I B O I S I S K
Y Z J B F M U C T S N P N S Y
L Z F A K K Q K S H N E C E X
S E S O R Y U E R M I L E N T
M W P K D C S D L C N L S D M
S N R O H T A P A D G T S N A
C M I U D F H S E O N Z U I R
P H N N J N T F F E Q I R K R
X C C O L L G Z E E L Y P J I
T K E G E S O T V E G S H S A
I I P A U M X A F A I R Y M G
S S O R N I R K R Y F Y I W E
U S V D S B B L J X E A K S N
```

Beauty	King	Sixteen
Brave	Kiss	Sleep
Castle	Marriage	Spell
Dragon	Prince	Spindle
Fairy	Princess	Spinning
Good	Queen	Thorns
Kindness	Roses	Wicked

96 Animal space camp ↓↓↓

Match the missing parts and complete the image given below.

1
2
3
4
5

97 Guess this, genius! ↓↓↓

Rodney is bad at Math. Help him solve the two puzzles his teacher has given him.

If 2 = 6, 3 = 13, 4 = 20, 5 = 30, 6 = 42
then 9 = _____

If 12 + 12 = 9, 25 + 25 = 9, 18 + 18 = 81
then 29 + 29 =
_____

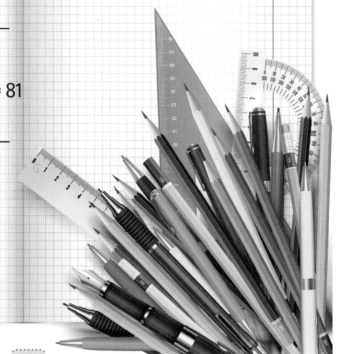

98 Bird in a cage

It's time to draw again! How about drawing a bird in a cage?
It could be a parrot or a lovebird... the choice is yours!

99 Odd one out

Can you spot the hidden cat among the dogs in less than a minute?

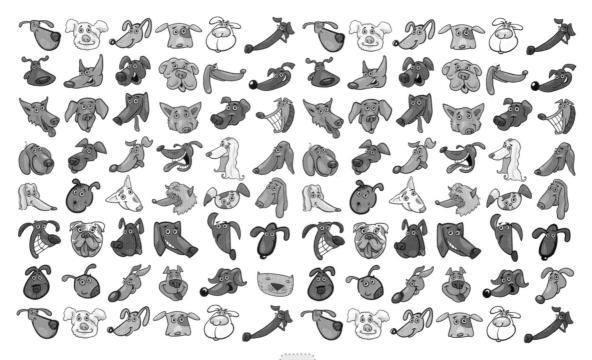

100 Addition hexagon

Each number in the second hexagon row is added to the two numbers below it.
Do the additions to get the number at the top.

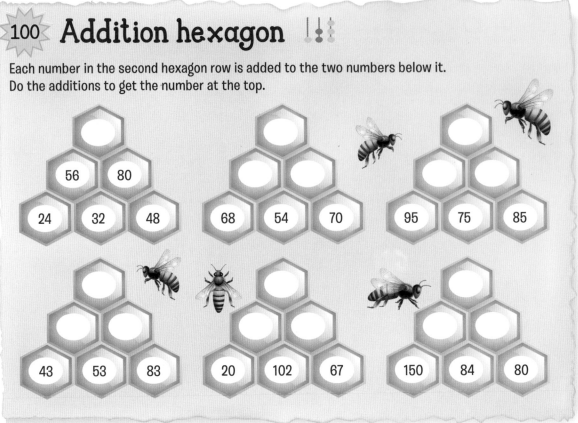

56   80

24   32   48

68   54   70

95   75   85

43   53   83

20   102   67

150   84   80

101 Wish the team good luck!

Change or remove a letter to move up the ladder!

Hint: The coach said to us, "Good ___, team!"

Hint: Past tense of wear

Hint: Ripped

Hint: An enormous weight: 2,000 pounds

Hint: What you pay to cross a bridge

Hint: Opposite of short

Hint: A story

Hint: Get or bring something

Hint: Opposite of wild

Team

102 Pre-historic maze

Help the caveboy reach the set of eggs safely through the maze.

103 For pet's sake!

Decode the different breeds of dogs.

 + = _____

 + +  = _____

+ a _____ of three + ER = _____

 + mation = _____

104 Something fishy

Cut square pieces of paper, use a tracing paper to mark out the shapes and use the cut out shapes to make the fish.

105 Tropical jungle

Find as many differences as you can in the images below.

106 Hobbies and interests

People have different hobbies and interests. Can you find the ones hidden in this puzzle?

Across:
1. To help a social cause
2. To design with tiles
3. To go on a journey
4. Interest in vintage cars, old books etc.

Down:
1. Interest in films
2. To do vocals in a choir
3. A form of exercise
4. To meet new people
5. To makes things using different art materials

107 A to Z animals

Let's make flash cards for your friends or sibling about the animals around the world.

Materials required: 26 rectangular sheets of card paper of size 2.5x3.5 cms, sketch pens, glue, images representing the animals from a to z

Method:
1. On each of the 26 sheets of card paper, write an alphabet from A to Z.
2. On the other side, draw or paste images of the animals that start with the same letter. The level is medium so try and avoid using cat or dog and instead try chameleon or cheetah.
3. Once done, shuffle the cards and play with friends or family.

108 Guess what Goldie ate?

Have you read the famous story about Goldilocks? Then you are sure to get this right! Make as many words using two or more letters. Make sure that every word uses the highlighted word in the center. Make one word using all the letters.

_____

_____

_____

_____

_____

_____

109 Airport diaries

Maya just went to drop off her favourite aunt Lucy at the airport.
Complete the picture so she can add it to her diary.

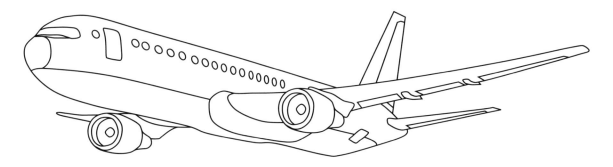

110 Who lives under the rocks in the sea?

Add, change, replace or remove one letter or more to go from SEA to EEL.

	Hint: A creature that lives under rocks in the sea
	Hint: You ____ a banana
	Hint: Dinner or lunch is a ____
	Hint: A shade of green
	Hint: To fasten or close something securely
Sea	

111 Rainbow spaghetti

Turn boring food into a colourful rainbow!
To make rainbow spaghetti, here's what you will need.

Materials required: One packet of spaghetti, food colouring, water, pot for boiling water, zip lock bags

Method:
1. Get an adult to help you put some spaghetti on to cook.
2. While it's cooking, put two teaspoons of each food colour that you have in different zip lock bags.
3. Add a few drops of water to each bag and shake to mix into the food colour.
4. When the spaghetti is cooked, cool it and put a little into each bag. Let it absorb the colour.
5. Drain the water - your rainbow spaghetti is ready to be eaten!

112 Get to the top

Add, replace or remove a letter or more to move to the next step of the pyramid.

S H A N D Y

H O N E S T

113 Game on!

Find the list of sports played with a ball across the globe.

List of games:
1. Dodgeball
2. Golf
3. Lacrosse
4. Bowling
5. Baseball
6. Cricket
7. Wiffleball
8. Handball
9. Netball
10. Snooker
11. Pool
12. Football
13. Basketball
14. Volleyball
15. Squash
16. Softball
17. Tennis
18. Polo

```
O S B N V O L L E Y B A L L
L Q A E L L A B T F O S T O
L U S T A G B P A L A O E P
A A A B L O O B O R N S K A
B S S A I L B E N L O L C S
E H N L Y F L L R F O P I C
S A L L A B E G D O D O R N
A L C H A N D B A L L L C B
B U N F O O T B A L L O S O
W F B F L A C R O S S E L W
L F L L A B E L F F I W N L
A S B A S K E T B A L L L I
S I N N E T P O O L B H L N
L D N A B C S N O O K E R G
```

114 Think about it

Read the question below and write down how you would solve it. Put a coin into an empty bottle and insert a cork into its neck. Is there a way to remove the coin without taking out the cork or breaking the bottle?

_____

_____

_____

115 Fun with patterns

Add another row of dots. Count all the dots to figure out the next number in the sequence. Then draw those many dots in the given space below. Write the number in the blanks as well.

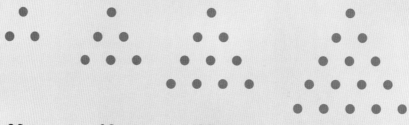

1 Dot   3 Dots   6 Dots   10 Dots   15 Dots

_____

116 **Your bedroom**

What does your bedroom look like? Draw it in the space given below.

117 Decode the secret message

Mr Tums is a secret agent and has sent a coded message to Mrs Baker, an old lady who works at an old patisserie. She can't figure out the message and wants help. Go ahead, decode old Mrs Baker's message so that she knows what is going on!

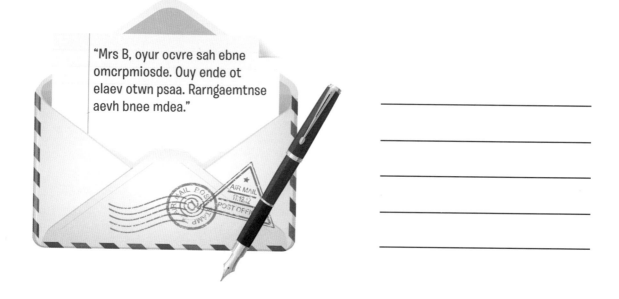

"Mrs B, oyur ocvre sah ebne omcrpmiosde. Ouy ende ot elaev otwn psaa. Rarngaemtnse aevh bnee mdea."

_____

_____

_____

_____

_____

118 Life on another planet

Complete the picture by colouring it as per the number clues.

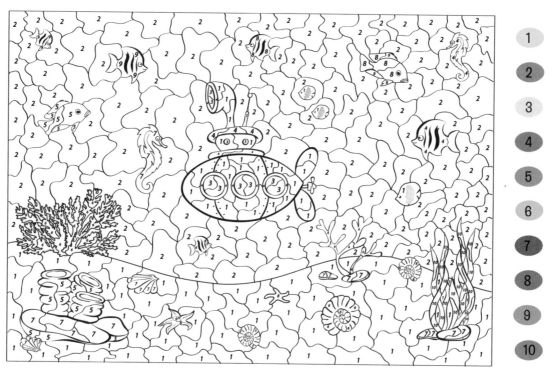

119 Upcycled book planter

Ask your parents for the old books that no one reads any more. It's time to upcycle them and transform waste into stuff you want to keep!

Materials required: Old books, scissors, glue, paints, small planter

Method:

1. Find four or five books that can be cut - ask an adult for help with the scissors!
2. Stack them up, one on top of the other. First stick two together to make your base. It should be strong and not wobbly.
3. Then make a circular hole in the middle of each of the other books. This should be big enough to set a circular planter inside.
4. Stick the cut books together. You can paint the books, if you like, in whatever colours and designs you want to.
5. Remember, once the paint is dry, place the planter inside and voila! Your pretty little upcycled book planter is ready to be shown off!

120 Late for tuition

Read the question below and guess the answer.

Rose has math tuition every Saturday evening. While leaving the house, she looks at the clock in the mirror. The clock has no number indication on it. She makes a mistake in reading time through the clock's reflection. Rose quickly cycles to her tuition, but arrives twenty minutes late. The clock at her tuition shows a time that is two hours later than the time that Rose saw on the clock at home. Guess the time on her clock at home and what the actual time at the tuition was.

121 Icecapades

Penguins, polar bears, seals and sea lions are just some animals you can find in the Arctic and Antarctic regions. Look at the images given below and see if you can find at least 10 differences in them.

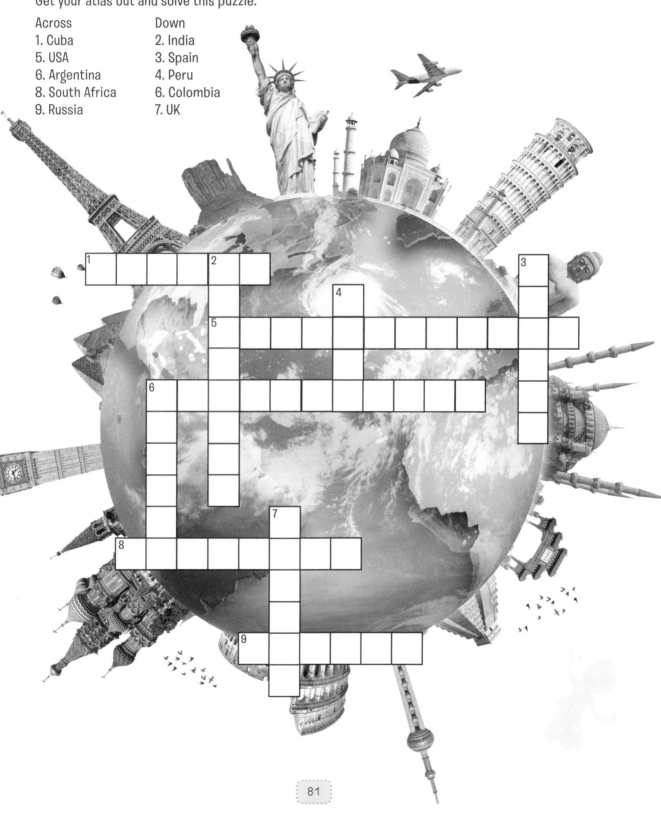

122 Capitals of countries around the world 🎵🎶

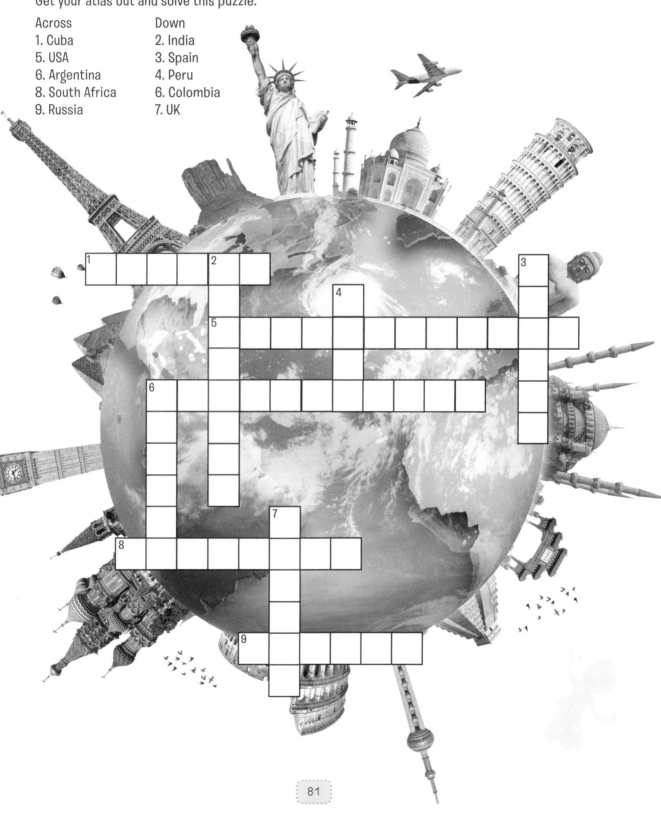

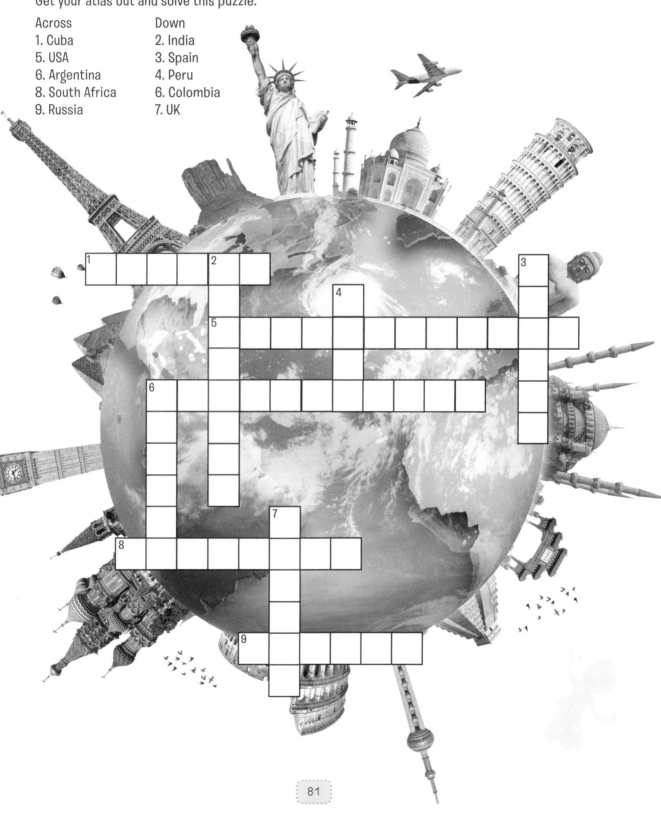
Marvellous May!

Do you know what the capital of these countries are?
Get your atlas out and solve this puzzle.

Across
1. Cuba
5. USA
6. Argentina
8. South Africa
9. Russia

Down
2. India
3. Spain
4. Peru
6. Colombia
7. UK

123 Water wonderland

Summer is all about fun in the sun and going away to the beach or sunbathing at the poolside. This jumbo slide maze requires you to go from point 1, 2, 3, 4 & 5 and reach point A, B, C, D or E. Can you find which path leads to the end?

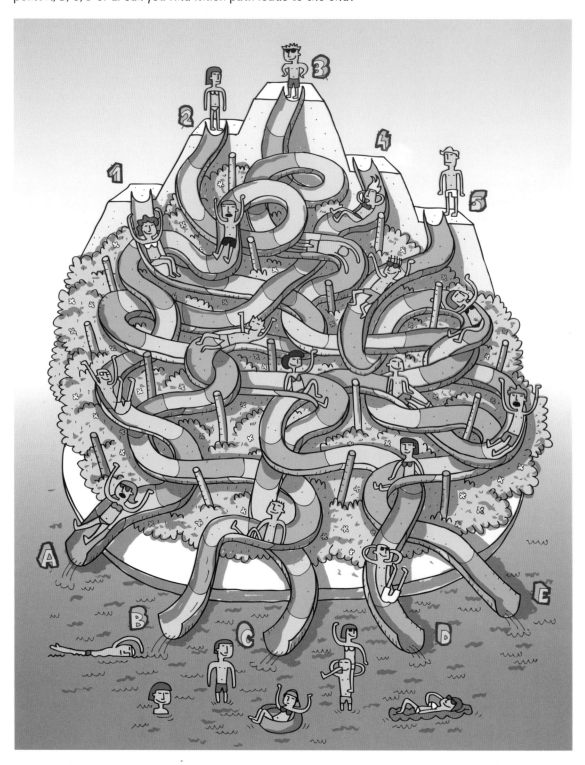

124 What do you see?

Look at the image for a few minutes and figure out what you see.
Write in the space below.

_____

_____

_____

125 Everybody loves art

Replace, add or remove one letter or more to move up the ladder!

Hint: Place to display art that starts with G

Hint: Everyone and everything

Hint: An enclosed shopping center

Hint: Opposite of short

Hint: To speak

Hint: A little nail for hanging things

Hint: What you do with a suitcase

Hint: A place for recreation

Hint: A ____ of something

Art

126 Abstract act

Replace or remove some of the letters to finally reach a single letter.

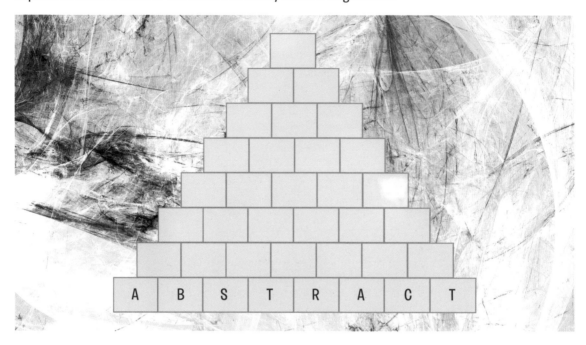

| A | B | S | T | R | A | C | T |

127 An aquarium at the restaurant

Do you know the seven best underwater restaurants?

Across:
2. A sea creature that is also a sun sign
3. An eight-legged sea creature
4. Sea stars
5. The term "jelly-like" comes from these creatures

Down:
1. A red ten-legged sea crustacean

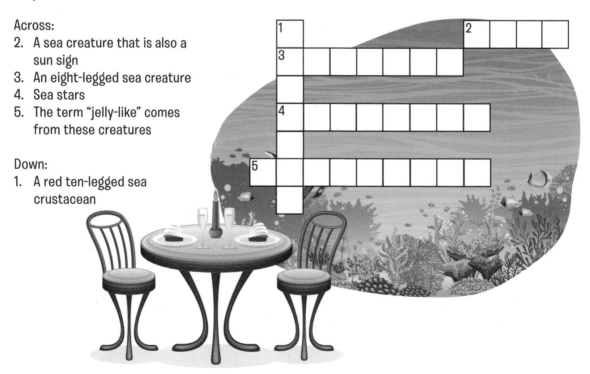

128 Pizza mania

You love pizzas and the toppings that come with them. Use the plate to create a pizza loaded with whatever you like best!

129 Doubts about the dots

Take a look at the boxes below and guess what the missing box would be. Be sure to look at the answer options below too!

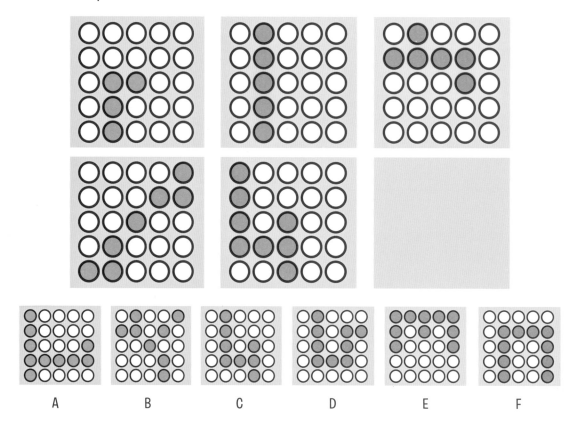

A   B   C   D   E   F

130 Nin, Rin and the Teepee

Look at the picture given below and spot the differences.

131 Catch the dream

Make as many words as you can think of using the letters in the wheel. Every word must use the letter in the middle. Try and make one word using all the letters.

_____

_____

_____

_____

_____

_____

_____

132 Reading with the family

Grandma Sue and her family love reading together. Look at the image carefully and find the hidden words!

_____

_____

_____

_____

_____

_____

133 Frolicking leapers ⏐⏐⏐

Join the dots and colour the image below to complete the picture.

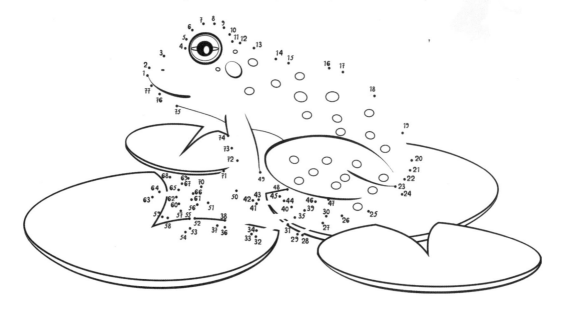

134 Stone age sudoku ⏐⏐⏐

The rules of the game are simple. There are 81 squares, each divided into nine blocks containing nine squares. Each block contains the numbers one to nine. Each number can appear only once in a row, column or box.

1		6	2	5			4	8
				8	9			
4		9	3	6		1		
3		4		8				
		8			3			4
9				3	4	6		5
2				7	6	8	9	3
8								7
6				4				1

135 Dessert frenzy

Chef Annie is livid. Her intern Lucy messed up the sign boards with randomly spelled out desserts for the day. Help Chef Annie unjumble the spellings on the board.

ercme ed al cmree
aisretispe slspacie

1. ltecohoca
2. issantcros
3. wrerysbart fletruf
4. mirastui
5. ochco tysarp
6. albkc rtefso

_____

_____

_____

_____

_____

_____

_____

136 Make it at home – Water lamp!

Instead of using candles, use water in this easy-to make and interesting lamp.

Materials required: A glass, water, some oil and a wick

Method: Pour up to 3/4th quantity of the water into the glass. Then pour in 2-4 tablespoons of oil and set the wick in the middle of the glass. The oil will float, because water and oil do not mix. This ensures that the wick stays dry and lasts longer.

137 Butterfly, fly away ↓↓↓

Find the matching patterns of the butterflies in the image below.

138 Monsters mania ↓↓↓

There are so many monsters running around the streets! Count the number of monsters in the image.

139 Precious stones

Solve this puzzle to find the different precious gems hidden inside!

Across:
1. They say you can see the moon on this stone
2. They are a girl's best friend
3. A glassy purple stone
4. A shade of green
5. A pink stone that shares the name with a flower

Down:
1. It is the name of a shade of green-blue
2. A precious blue gemstone
3. Replace one letter in the word oval
4. A famous and precious stone used in carving the Chinese ____ Cabbage

140 Test your IQ

Look at the images carefully and figure out which numbered shape will come next.

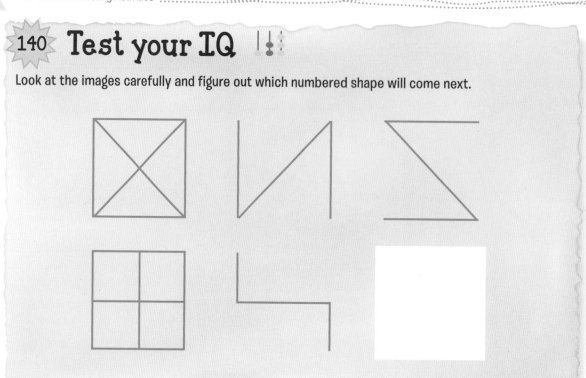

141 Types of clouds

When you look into the sky, what kinds of clouds do you see? Look at the list below and find the different clouds in this puzzle.

```
K W U J V W W R J V R Y H D S C V U
I A J M L K Q C H T P W Q Y I J Z G
T Z K W A G P K G Z U R O S G W P C
H W I D C U M U L U S T Y B A Q C D
E Y U S V C I R R O C U M U L U S M
G D B L F H H Z O L L T J T J Z E Y
O D K H A T K Z J J N T W N M E S P
Y W Q V B O G K A J Z G L A S U J B
G J R V X V C R T X C Q N Z T P W W
S T R A T O C U M U L U S A V M V U
Z D E D C I A V D B S X R N S G I Q
H U P M Y G P B Z Q R T U Y N E J X
K E D V J N Y S I B S S T S A A F Q
N C E Z M N H H V E V O B S Y J L
N N I M B O S T R A T U S Q T I O U
R R U S W C M R D R O D Q S R P F H
H W U N R X I A L T O S T R A T U S
R H L B W C L I B B M V R T Y Z Z
E Q K T J T B Q Z R O G W B U E W Z
X J L M Y C I R R U S U N Z S X P P
```

1. Cirrostratus
2. Cirrus
3. Cirrocumulus
4. Nimbostratus
5. Altostratus
6. Stratus
7. Stratocumulus
8. Cumulus

142 Upcycled mosaic

A mosaic is a type of art that is usually made with broken tiles. Today, you will learn how to make a mosaic using different bottle caps.

Materials required: As many bottle/jar caps as you can find, glue/adhesive, a 10 x 15 cm canvas board and a pencil

Method:
1. On the canvas, draw the outline of a scene using your pencil. It could be an underwater scene like in the picture or something entirely from your imagination.
2. Get an adult to help if you need.
3. Once you've drawn the outline, decide where you want to use big caps and where you want to use small ones.
4. Start sticking on the caps using glue, placing them exactly where you planned to.
5. Try and use as many colours as possible, so your mosaic looks pretty and bright.
6. Complete the entire piece in the same way and keep it aside for 24 hours to dry. You have a work of art to show off!

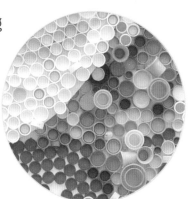

143 In the jungle

Spot at least seven differences in the jungle scenes!

144 Classroom madness

Help Regina solve a math quiz assigned by her teacher! Fill the blanks with numbers
1 to 9 without repeating a number.

	+	1	+		=	9
+		+		+		
	+		+	8	=	18
+		+		+		
9	+		+		=	18
=		=		=		
18		9		18		

145 Clear blue skies

Can you solve these hints about
a beautiful clear day?

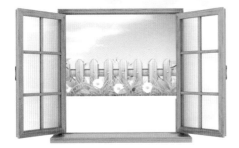

Hint: A _____ full of stars	
Hint: "As ____ as a fox"	
Hint: A common winged insect	
Hint: The river waters ____ south	
Hint: A tiny insect	
Hint: To run away from danger	
Hint: Synonym for happiness or joy	
Hint: Substance used to stick things together	
Hint: Another for hint	
	Blue

146 Life on Mars

Complete the image by looking at the colours given below and filling it in.

147 Out of this world

Can you find your way in and around this maze?

148 Number 23

Can you find five consecutive numbers that add up to 23?

9 4 7 2 5 1 7 3 9 2 4 4 5 7 2 5 6 1 8 5 4

149 Gorgeous garden flowers

Draw a garden in full bloom.

150 Let's go fishing

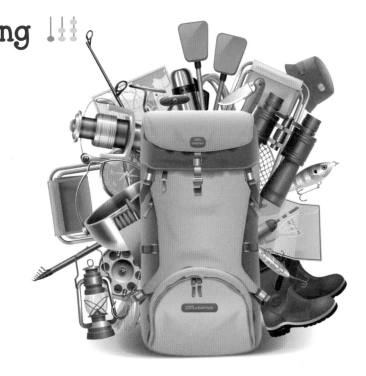

Get ready to go hunting for that fishing gear.

How to play: Your dad wants to take you fishing, so before you both set off, he wants you to recognise the different equipment used during this sport. He hands you a list of things you need to find in and around the house.

151 The world of insects

Can you find the different types of insects hidden in this puzzle?

```
G D I D B D T E I G C O C O O N Y W
C F P E V R V T A Y B Q I B C T X F
O Z F I R E F L Y N R L N H M K B E
A D R A G O N F L Y P L S Q Y W E U
P J A T E R M I T E R C C V W B E K
G Z M S X A V G Q T A O T L N U T E
S L O Z H C F C S I Y C T A N T L R
I G S U V G L E O S I K P D R T E P
X J Q B E E J I R L N R U Y L E F K
Q Y U N R E G F O E G O I B K R I Y
B P I C R I C K E T M A V U P F Q X
U U T K X F L E A M A C Z G B L N V
P N O A T J U G K A N H P E R Y N M
H O R S E F L Y Q Q T M D L B P P O
T H G L O W A N T P I E Z D Q O H T
O N W A A D G N D H S P I B B F O H
T G H G R A S S H O P P E R F N T L
```

Ant	Flea
Bee	Moth
Beetle	Praying Mantis
Butterfly	Termite
Cockroach	Grasshopper
Cocoon	Horsefly
Cricket	Ladybug
Dragonfly	Mosquito

152 Tickle your brain

Look at the boxes below and see if you can figure out what phrases these images suggest.

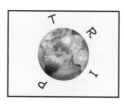

153 Draw your favourite character

Get your pencils, colours and paints out, because it's time to draw your favourite character from any story.

154 A roller coaster ride

Josh, Ferdinand, Rex and Cameron love going on a roller coaster ride! But during the ride, they notice some missing numbers on the tracks. Can you help them figure out which numbers are missing?

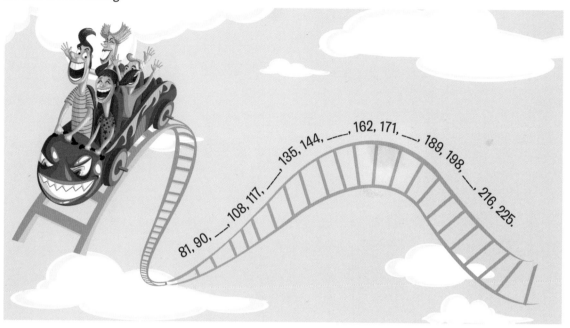

81, 90, ——, 108, 117, ——, 135, 144, ——, 162, 171, ——, 189, 198, ——, 216, 225.

155 Paisley print

Doodle the one that comes next.

_____

_____

Popsicle photo frame

Bring out your favourite photographs and make a lovely frame for you to display them!

Materials required: 15 popsicle sticks, glue, paints, scissors, photographs, thumb tacks, craft paper

Method:
1. Glue eight popsicle sticks together. Leave them to dry for a few hours.
2. Paint them in any colour you like. Let them dry again.
3. Place the photograph on the frame to see how much of the photo you need to cut off. You should be left with some blank space on one side of the frame.
4. Once you have an estimate, take out the picture. Use the excess space on the frame to stick pretty shapes that you can cut out of craft paper.
5. Keep it aside for a few hours and then pin the photograph to the frame. You can use two more tacks and a piece of string to hang the frame on the wall or on your softboard.

157 Sudoku Samurai

Samurai Xi Tao has been told to fill in this puzzle before his final test. Help him finish his task!

	7	8				3	9	
4			7		2			5
6		3	1		8	4		7
	1	2	8		3	9	7	
				5				
	8	6	2		1	5	3	
1		9	4		6	7		3
8			3		7			9
	3	4				2	6	

158 Adventures on the safari

Imagine that you are in a jeep in a wonderful jungle in Africa. Can you draw pictures of the safari and the different animals that you saw?

159 ## Somewhere in space

Look at the image carefully to find the hidden words.

 160 ## Box of matches

Change the shape of the grid by removing 9 matchsticks. Make sure no squares are left.

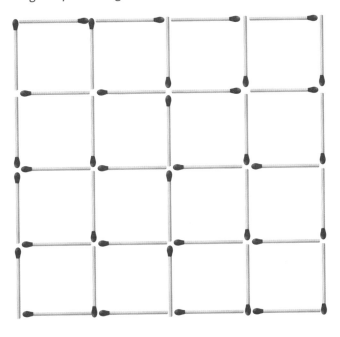

161 Sail on!

How about you build your own little paper boat tangram? Cut square pieces of paper, trace out the shapes and cut accordingly.
Use the cut out shapes to construct your boat.

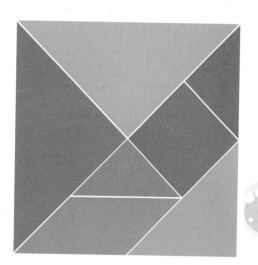

162 Cross number

You've done crosswords before, but have you done a cross number? Try one!
Look at the clues given - you need to simply do some addition to get your answers!

Across:
1. 12 + 26
3. 4342 + 4375
7. 486 + 250
9. 1285 + 2275
10. 15 + 802
12. 3 + 37
13. 2 + 12
14. 24 + 111
15. 325 + 490
17. 30 + 17
18. 3 + 31
19. 52 + 396
20. 509 + 6522
22. 63 + 711
25. 4192 + 2735
26. 7 + 54

Down:
1. 16 + 21
2. 28 + 55
3. 351 + 486
4. 15 + 60
5. 665 + 978
6. 2361 + 4644
8. 2576 + 4239
11. 3 + 11
14. 51 + 1736
15. 2783 + 5593
16. 545 + 884
17. 8 + 36
19. 229 + 188
21. 8 + 24
23. 18 + 58
24. 22 + 19

163 Twisted logic

Help Ron figure out what number replaces the question mark.

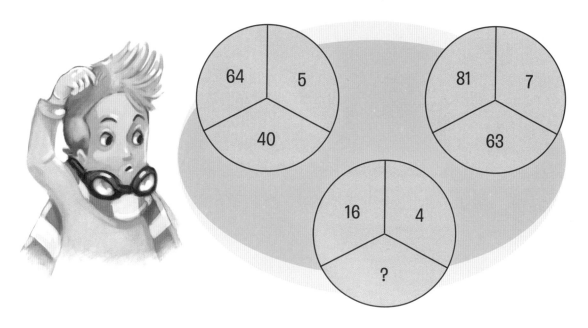

164 Time for desserts

Turn your friend's favourite desserts into a set of flashcards that you both can play with it.

Materials required: 10 rectangular card paper sheets of size 2.5cms x 3.5cms, pencil, eraser, ruler, sketches, glue, images of your friend's favourite desserts

Method:
1. On one side of the cards, draw or stick 10 images of your friend's favourite desserts.
2. On the other side of each card, write down their name of the dessert. You can use the given example to see how to decorate the card.

165 Fruity garden

Do you know your fruits and berries well enough? If yes, try and guess the names of the fruits and berries arranged around the puzzle and write them down! You could ask an adult for help if you need it!

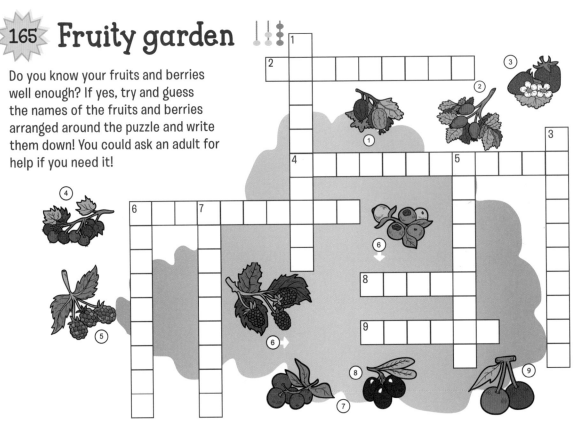

166 Clock work

Match the different minutes on the right to the corresponding alphabets on the clock to the left.

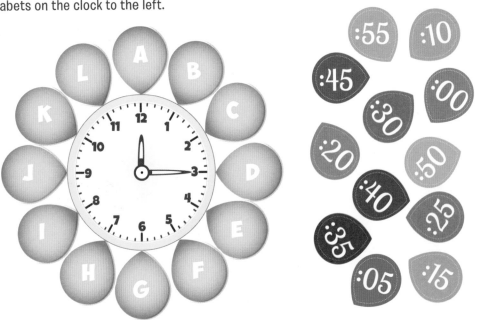

167 Days of the dinos ⌡⌡⌡

Rewind back in time to the days when dinosaurs roamed the earth. Add a background to the picture and colour it as you imagine life was at that time!

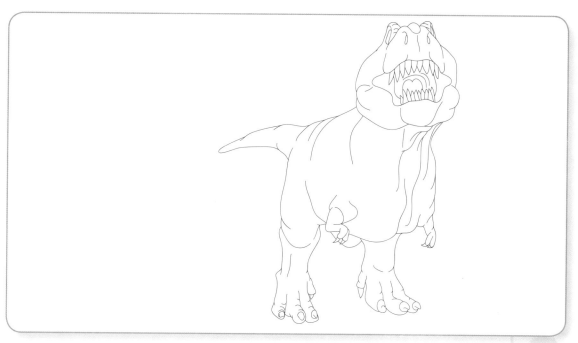

 168 Sweater weather ⌡⌡⌡

Add, remove or change one letter or more to go up the ladder!

Hint: What changes every three months and goes from hot to cold?

Hint: Past perfect of beat

Hint: Past perfect tense of eat

Hint: Add more sugar to _____ something

Hint: Opposite of sour

Hint: Perspiration

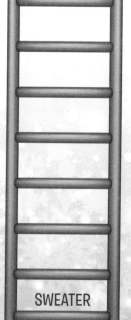

SWEATER

169 Up, up and away!

Change or remove one letter from the last word to go up the pyramid!

B

B A L L O O N

B

S O A R I N G

170 The Egyptian beetle

Draw the image on the right, exactly the same way on to the left. Use a pencil to complete it, then colour it with crayons or paint.

171 Design by lines ♩♪♪

Can you guess how many squares have been used in this design?

172 The family pack ♩♪♪

It's always fun playing cards with the family. Here is how you can make your own set of playing cards.

Materials required: Pencil, eraser, ruler, sketch pens, 12 rectangular sheets of card paper (each measuring 2.5" x 3.5") and a pack of playing cards for reference

Method:
1. On one side of the card papers, write A, 2, 3, 4, 5, 6, 7, 8, 9, 10, J, Q and K.
2. One the other side, draw doodles of your family members first with a pencil, then colour them with the sketch pens.
3. Add in doodles of your favourite aunt, uncle and cousin too. Also, don't forget to draw a doodle of yourself as well!

173 The snake charmer

The snake charmer's music has got the snakes all tangled up! Figure out which snake belongs to which basket.

174 Detective Gordie saves the day!

Gordie, the city detective, has been assigned an interesting case which requires him to solve a few clues. Help him solve the clues and crack the case.

Clue # 1 - Guess this to figure out what the case is about.

Clue # 2 Guess what was missing from the place where the crime occurred.

175 # The girl in the red hood

Remember the story of Little Red Riding Hood? Find words from that fairytale in the puzzle below!

```
Q S U M Z D G W Y P Q L X L B
G G R A N D M O T H E R I C K
K G E S J X I O D G T J Q I N
M N H U X W F D A B T D T G R
K N S Q D S C S F Q V Y H A U
D T W U G L C J N A A R I P Q
M R O I S D N H N P L Q E U D
D E O V B L T B J I I L N O V
B D D E N W C L G L D T O K J
Y K C R Z T Q N K W Z H P Q K
Y C U I T B I C A J I W L B L
E U T N T D A D N G A S Q T T
I E T G I S F D A C D Q Z W L
X O E R J Q W O L F J W T H Y
A K R G J Z P S D B C U X E R
```

1.	Red	6.	Grandmother
2.	Riding	7.	Woodcutter
3.	Hood	8.	Woods
4.	Bad	9.	Quivering
5.	Wolf	10.	Dawdle

 176 # Drink up!

Add, replace or remove one letter or more to go from POP to SODA!

Hint: Another name for a fizzy drink _____

Hint: Grass attached to earth _____

Hint: Unhappy _____

Hint: Short for Sidney _____

Hint: What you do in a chair _____

Hint: Saliva _____

Hint: A hole in the ground _____

Hint: An animal that lives in a house _____

Hint: Lots of energy _____

Pop

177 The animal pack

Make your own set of cards to play with your friends. Use animals as your first theme!

Materials required: Pencil, eraser, ruler, sketches, 12 rectangular sheets of card paper (each measuring 2.5" x 3.5"), a pack of playing cards for reference

Method:

1. Use one paw print design from the options given below on each card to complete your animal pack of cards.
2. You can either use them on the number side or just on the top.

LION BOAR WOLF GIRAFFE
HIPPOPOTAMUS BEAR DEER FERRET
JAGUAR ELEPHANT CHICKEN CAT
KANGAROO CAMEL FOX SQUIRREL

178 The amusement park

Guess the things that you will see in an amusement park, in the crossword below.

Across

2. A giant wheel on which you can sit and go round and round
6. Pink sugar clouds that are edible
7. Part of the playground that requires you to walk up the stairs but _____ to come down
8. A ride that turns upside down
9. A ride that goes 'Toot Toot!'

Down

1. Buttery corn kernels heated
3. A room where your reflection is distorted
4. A tricky path that takes you from start to finish
5. Comedians, clowns, dancers and acrobats do different _____

179 How many dogs?

Can you tell how many dogs there are in the picture?

180 Cute pets

Write the names of these pets by looking at their images.

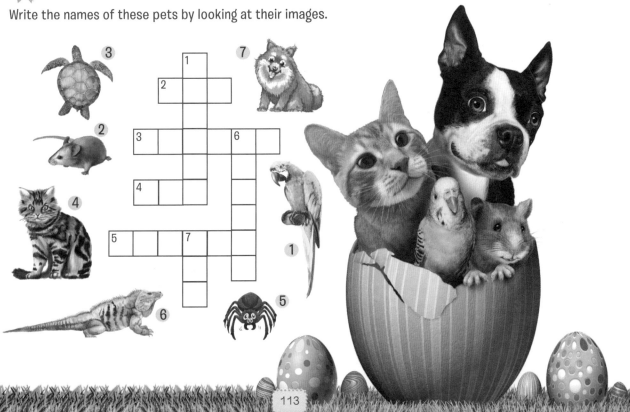

181 Out in the garden

Use your artistic skills to colour this garden scene!

182 Parking problems

Look at the image below and try and figure out what number the car is parked on.

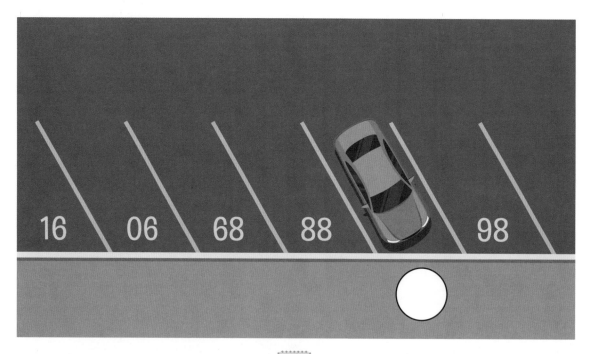

16   06   68   88   98

Change, add or remove one letter or more to go up the ladder.

	Hint: I listened to the game on the _____
	Hint: A comparison of two amounts using division.
	Hint: A large rodent.
	Hint: You wear this on your head.
	Hint: This makes something hot.
	Hint: Something that you sit on.
	Hint: A collection of related items.
	Hint: To be seated.
	Hint: To pay a _____ someone.
	Hint: The sense of sight.
Television	

184 The colour game ⁝

Look at the image for a few minutes and try pronouncing the COLOUR instead of the WORD. The right hemisphere of your brain is trying to pronounce the colour, while the left hemisphere insists on pronouncing the word.

BLUE GREEN YELLOW BLUE
RED BLACK BLUE
YELLOW BLUE RED GREEN
BLACK YELLOW GREEN

185 Peter in Neverland ⁝

Ask your parent to tell you the story of Peter Pan and his adventures. Then try and solve this easy crossword puzzle.

Across
1. The man with one hand.

Down
1. The eldest daughter of the Darlings family.
2. The youngest of the Darlings.
3. The pixie fairy and Peter's friend.
4. Capt. Hook's nemesis is a saltwater

186 Shadow game

Can you find this cute puppy's shadow?

187 Rory's gifts!

It's Rory's birthday and she's excited to see her gifts. Help her open them by finding the right ribbons to pull.

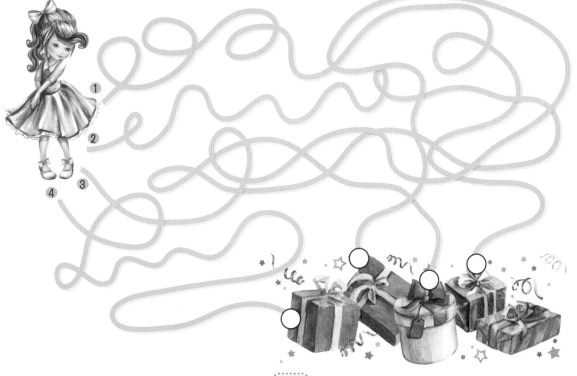

188 Baker's dozen!

Find the hidden words that are related to baking!

```
Z M A M Z T G U C G D U Q Y U
E T T E U G A B B F B R E A M M
T O B S W O W U R K I T G X U
G D W P A N C A K E S X P H F
O J I U S N F J H A C L O A F
W A F F L E D G P Y U R B E I
Q B Q S L R U W O W I C E U N
R U W U Z O G F C U T M N A U
P R T C D B U I E O G P L X M
V G C U R P U R E S O H C F E
S E J W Z W A V U F E K N M V
B R U S C H E T T A K W I U Y
D R G A P G R Q D B U T T E R
D F F U E D M R C R O L L S W
U L C R O I S S A N T H C P O
```

cream, cookie
dough, croissant
rolls, waffle,
pancakes,
muffin, loaf,
burger, biscuit,
bruschetta,
baguette,
butter, flour

189 A teen's world

Find up to 13 differences in the two scenes below.

190 Next in line

Solve this logic question.
What comes in place of the question mark in the following series?

WE SG PJ LN [?]

HS IT IS HT
①   ②   ③   ④

191 Camping under the stars

Bring out your colour pencils and make a drawing about camping under the stars.

192 Try this triangle test

Fill in the numbers from 1 to 6. Ensure that each side of the triangle adds up to 9, without repeating a number.

193 Captain Crook

Help the captain hide his treasure on a secret island. Which route do you think he should choose?

194 Non-toxic play dough

Here's a do-it-yourself activity to make play dough at home. The best part is, it takes just 10 minutes! Make sure that there is an adult to help you.

Materials required: 1 cup flour, 1 cup water, 2 teaspoons cream of tartar, 1 large container, 1/3 cup salt, 1 tablespoon vegetable oil and food colouring

Method:
1. In a saucepan, add the flour, cream of tartar and salt.
2. Add in the water and 1 tablespoon of oil.
3. Turn the burner on medium/low and keep stirring till it becomes a bit lumpy.
4. Keep stirring post that as well till it starts becoming solid.
5. On a heated pan, it should take 20-30 seconds but a minute or 2 otherwise.
6. When it starts solidifying, add the food colouring (a little goes a long way). It will get lumpier and thicker but keep stirring.
7. If the dough starts gathering, it means it's ready.
8. Remove from the pan and pour it on the parchment or wax paper to cool.
9. Knead it out for a few minutes just to better its consistency.
10. Your home made play dough is ready!

195 Such a cosmopolitan world!

Make as many two or more letter words using the highlighted letters. Make sure in every word you use the letter in the middle. Make one word using all the letters.

N C S M O O T P L I O A

_____

_____

_____

_____

_____

_____

_____

_____

196 Into the woods

Find seven hidden words in this image.

Precious pattern

Look at the images below and figure out which two match. Notice every little detail.

1
2
3
4
5
6

198 Where do they belong?

Can you match the people to their respective homes?

199 Message in a bottle ⁞⁞⁞

While Lucas was sitting by the beach, a bottle was washed ashore. To his surprise, the bottle had a cryptic message inside. Help him figure out what the message said.

"ytado oyu rea you, htat si uretr naht eurt. Erthe si on eon ivale how si yreuo hant ouy" Dr Seuss.

_____

_____

_____

200 Your favourite toy ⁞⁞⁞

Turn your favourite toy into a painting with shadow painting.

Materials required: Your favourite toy, pencil, eraser, paints, table lamp

Method:
1. Place your toy under a light so you see its shadow on the page or on a paper.
2. Take a pencil and draw the outline after which you can keep aside the toy. You can keep looking at it for reference but the fun is in completing the painting on your own.
3. If your toy is a teddy bear, you can paint the entire thing in black like a silhouette and just highlight its accessories like a scarf or a tie. You can even give it a background of your choice.

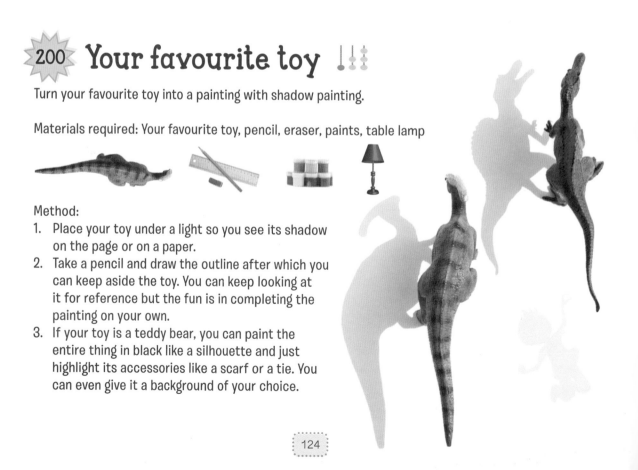

201 Out in the desert

Name all the wildlife you can see in this scene.
What time do you think it is?

202 Howzzat

Look for the words related to cricket in the word search below.

```
E B F I E L D I N G F C
S L O C A T C H A B P O
L B S U B A T S M A N I
I W P B N C F O U T R N
P I I C A D U C K T U N
N C N E Z T A W C I N I
A K W L O V E R S N S N
P E I E B A L L Y G Z G
P T D V Z C S T U M P S
E S E E C R I C K E T C
A G E N L P T E A M S A
L Z S M B O W L E R R P
```

Appeal	L.B.W	Slip	Cricket
Stumps	Out	Wicket	Catch
Batting	Cap	Eleven	Innings
Overs	Ball	Runs	Bat
Spin	Bowler	Fielding	Duck
Wide	Boundary	Teams	Batsman

CRICKET MANIA

203 Let's make a century!

Here's something to think about! The questions below are about 100. Try and figure out how.

How do you make a 100 using four sevens and a one?

_____

_____

How do you make a 100 using 60 and Ali Baba's thieves?

_____

_____

204 Gaga over gadgets

Try solving the puzzle below using the hints given.

Across
1. I ring and I text, I capture and I store. I am carried around everywhere you go. What am I?
2. I can sit when you sit, either on the floor or at the desk. I fold shut when not working. What am I?
3. Use me and you can see out into space. I am long, gold and have two sides to me. What am I?

Down
1. From one side, objects are closer. From the other, they are far. What am I?
2. I capture moments, faces and a lot of things on a paper. What am I?
3. What you see, I instantly capture and print. What am I?
4. When I stand on my three legs, I am the steadiest. What am I?
5. I am not a medicine, but I do carry the same name. I have a screen and am carried around wherever you go. What am I?

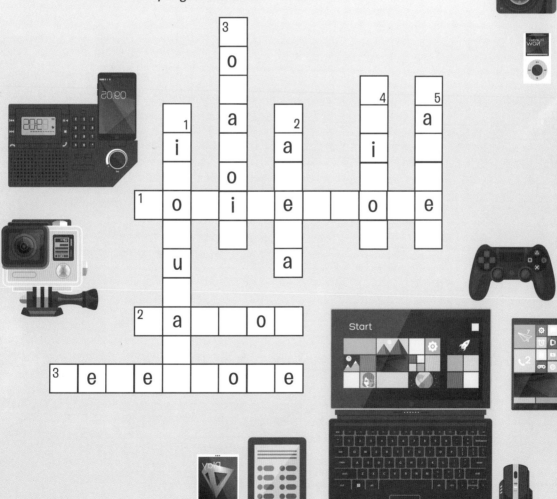

205 Out on the water ⁝⁝⁝

Join the dots and complete the image. You can paint or colour the rest of it!

206 Sudoku mania ⁝⁝⁝

Can you solve this sudoku puzzle?

2		🌙				6		
	4		8	7			⭐	2
8				⭐	🌙		4	
	3		7			8		⭐
	6	5			8		3	
⭐				3				7
			6	5		7		🌙
6		4					2	
	8		3		⭐	4	5	

207 Paper plane

Pilot the making of a paper plane tangram by cutting a square sheet into the shapes in the box to the right. Cut square pieces of paper, use a tracing paper to mark out the shapes. Cut accordingly. Put them together to build your paper plane.

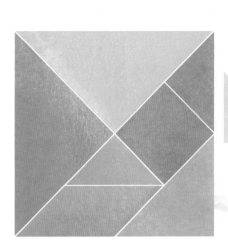

208 Thanksgiving lunch

Let's see if you can find the hidden words on this Thanksgiving table! Find nine of them.

209 Who am I?

Read the puzzle below and guess the right answer.

Drop my first letter;
Drop my second letter;
Drop all my letters and
I would remain the same.
Who am I?

_____

210 Landforms

Let's see if you can solve these pyramids using the landforms as a clue.

C O A S T A L

P L A T E A U

M O U N T A I N

211 Glass harmonicas

Ever thought of what it would sound like if you played music from glasses filled with water? How about you try it now.

Materials required: Five glasses of water, pencil

Method:
1. Take five glasses of water each filled at different levels.
2. The first one at the lowest and the last one with the most water.
3. Use a pencil and hit the glasses.
4. On doing that, each glass will react and make a different sound. Figure out which one makes the highest sound.

Do you know why they make the sound? It's because small vibrations are made every time you hit the glasses. It creates sound waves that travel through water and depending on the amount of water, the slower the vibrations and deeper the tone.

212 Popsicle stick harmonica ♪♪♪

Imagine making a music instrument from used popsicle sticks? Well, you can and here's how.

Materials required: Two popsicle sticks, two rubber bands, one long strip of paper and one toothpick

Method:
1. Take the long strip of paper and place it over one popsicle stick.
2. Place the other popsicle stick and secure it using one of the elastic bands on one side.
3. Once that's done, break the toothpick into half and push one half between the sticks near the secured end.
4. Hold the other end of the toothpick at the open end of the sticks. Then secure it again with the other elastic band.

If you have made a slight gap between the two sticks, then your harmonica is ready! Hold the sticks against your mouth and blow out air or draw in air till you hear sounds.

213 Let's go fly a kite ♪♪♪

Jack and Macy love flying kites. See how they have fun by colouring this image using the colour codes given.

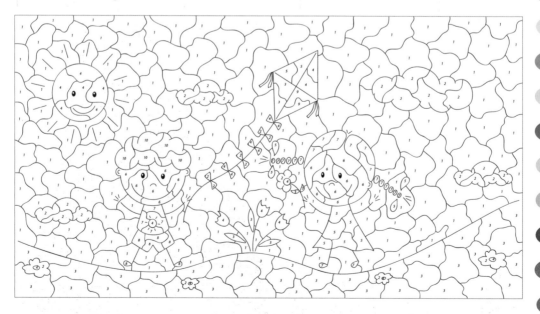

1
2
3
4
5
6
7
8
9
10

214 Time travel to Egypt

The list below has everything about ancient Egypt.
Take a look and circle the words you find.

```
E D A R T Y C L S N I Y L B T V Z X T
U K N A O R C A S O S P N R K B A X Z
N I S H D L T I P Y L S E S S E M A R
D N A S B E Q R N U M L J W Q Y S V I
Y G E Z E W L U J P U B E M G A C S W
R D L G T E Z B A R D O O L F R I U M
O O I T O J H P E G Y P T L D T H G U
T M T Z M L V Y O K L K G G Y A P A M
S V R L B R D M A S Q M D P N P Y H M
I Y E T U T A N K H A M U N A O L P Y
H Q F S A T B H H K S C M Y S E G O S
S J I C R F X T O I N Y E B T L O C A
L F S E V M T P H A J I S X Y C R R E
Y V S P B L G E Y T R G E S N I E A L
T E M P L E L U R R E A I D B I I S I
D O G X L V N O A L A S H E I O H R N
S V I Z I E R Z R T I M G P D C E P F
R B H F Q H I L M C Q F I K U E T H S
N O I T A G I R R I S M E D D K A M J
```

Afterlife	Jewellery	Giza	Sphinx
Ruler	Edict	History	Symbol
Burial	Kingdom	God	Temple
Ink	Egypt	Ramesses	Tomb
Cleopatra	Mummy	Reed	Trade
Nile	Fertile	Hieroglyphics	Tutankhamun
Desert	Pharaoh	History	Vizier
Irrigation	Flood	Sarcophagus	
Dynasty	Pyramid	Scroll	

215 Brothers and sisters

Can you answer this twisted logic question?

John and his brothers are one family.
Each brother has a sister.
How many sisters do they have?

_____

_____

_____

_____

216 Monster bookmark

All you bookworms, here's something for you to do today! Get some craft paper and let's make a monster bookmark! Look at the diagram below to learn how.

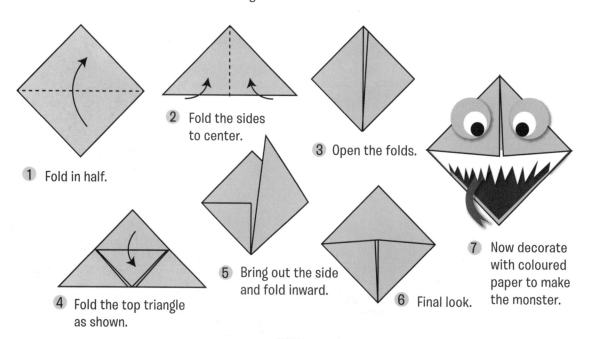

1 Fold in half.

2 Fold the sides to center.

3 Open the folds.

4 Fold the top triangle as shown.

5 Bring out the side and fold inward.

6 Final look.

7 Now decorate with coloured paper to make the monster.

217 Logic poem

The poem below spells out a word, letter by letter.
"The first" refers to the word's first letter and so on.
Let's see if you can figure out what the word is.

The first, is in fish but not in snail. _____

The second, in rabbit but not in tail. _____

The third, in up but not in down. _____

The fourth, in tiara not in crown. _____

The fifth, in a tree you plainly see. _____

The whole, a food for you and me. _____

_____

218 Aliens and spaceships

Use your imagination and draw an alien and its spaceship below.
You can use as many colours as you like.

219 Transport in the city

Guess the names of the different types of transport we use to travel or move things.

220 Four digits

What is the four-digit number in which the first digit is one-third the second, the third is the sum of the first and second, and the last is three times the second?

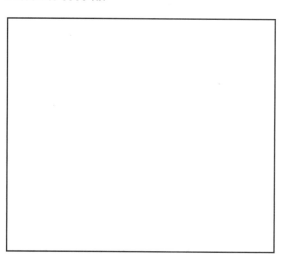

The tent by the river

Can you find 10 differences in the pictures of the village on the riverbank?

 # The intricate bird

Use lots of colours to make this bird beautiful.

223 Martin reads the paper ⌄⌄⌄

Every morning Martin reads the newspaper carefully. One day, the news seemed very weird. Can you help Martin make sense by rewriting the text?

Burglar clever how got the away.
No was behind left clue.
Was it reported as jewellery a theft. Prints fingers foot or marks show no of. Police house the looked entire through Mr Mrs and Morrison. Rich stayed old and in mansion couple a was it easy steal to anything. Reporter a witness.

_____

_____

_____

_____

_____

224 The bear and the honeypot ⌄⌄⌄

Complete the image and colour it too! Give it a background of your choice.

225 Mayan numericals

Guess the missing number in this number chart drawn by the mayans.

FIND THE NUMBERS
FROM 1 TO 25.
FIND THE MISSING NUMBER

3	25	6	13	9
7	10	2	23	16
12	18	?	4	21
1	22	14	11	19
8	20	5	17	15

226 Dogs around the world

Do you love dogs? Let's see if you can find the different breeds of dogs in the puzzle below.

```
S A I N T Y I B E A G L E Q A
F M L C C Q C D B J A B Y B G
S A H P H U F O A P U E M U S
R S A O I C S B S O O R N L H
O T S O H O V E S M B N Y L E
T I A D U L M R E E P A L D P
T F Y L A I M T R D R A O H
W F O E H I N A H A A D B G E
E T R U U E S N O N C W R S R
I P I D A P S O U I H T A C D
L P U G W U R F N A S E D W Y
E G E R M A N Q D N H F O G R
R T S H A R P P E I U B R P S
E A D A L M A T I A N C T V R
B O X E R G R E A T D A N E S
```

1. Basset Hound
2. Beagle
3. Boxer
4. Bulldog
5. Chihuahua
6. Collie
7. Dachshund
8. Dalmatian
9. Great Dane
10. Mastiff
11. Pomeranian
12. Poodle
13. Pug
14. Rottweiler
15. Sharp-Pei
16. Labrador
17. Doberman

227 Face time fun

How many faces can you create using the references below?

228 What topping would you like?

Here are some images that make up the name of a flavour/topping. Guess what they are!

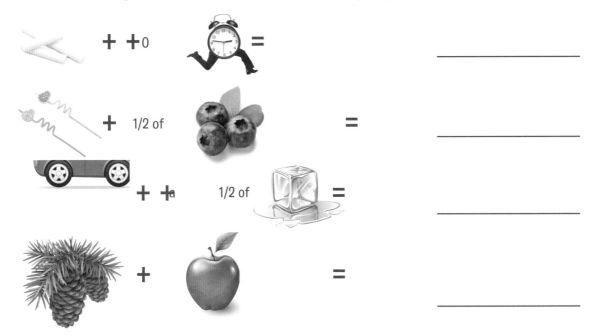

_____

+ +0 =

+ 1/2 of =   _____

+ +a 1/2 of =   _____

+ =   _____

229 The family room

Match the missing pieces to complete the image of Joyce's family room.

230 Time to clown around

Let's make some clown themed accessories today!

Materials required: Two paper plates, glue, egg carton, ribbon, paints, brushes, scissors, hole punching machine, newspaper

Method:

1. For the clown's collar - Start by drawing a circle on a paper plate. The edge of the plate should be two inches away from the circle. Use scissors to make a cut from the edge of the paper plate to the circle. Now cut out the circle. The ring that remains is the clown's collar. Paint dots on the collar. After the paint is dry, add more decorations if you like.

2. The clown's nose - Cut one section out of the egg carton. Punch a hole on each side and paint the whole thing red. This is the clown's nose. String a ribbon through the holes to tie the nose around your head.

3. The clown's hat - Take the second paper plate and fold it in half. Make a cut from the edge of the plate to the center of the plate. Overlap the two ends to form a cone. Ensure that it fits your head properly. Adjust it and staple the two ends of the cone to make a hat. Decorate it as you like.

4. The clown's hair - Paint a sheet of newspaper in bright orange and cut it into strips. Use glue to stick these on the sides of the clown's hat to make hair. Your clown hat is ready!

231 Fantasy land

Draw a fantasy theme background over the puzzle layout given below. Take a photocopy of the design and paste it on a cardboard sheet. Ensure you cut the pieces neatly and then you will have your own handmade puzzle!

232 Times Square

Guess how many squares there are in this image.

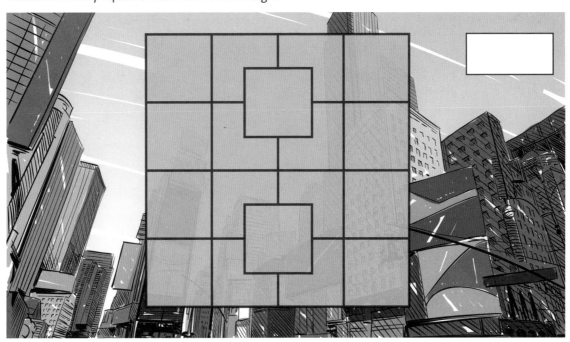

233 Cleo the clown fish

Join the dots to see what Cleo the clown fish looks like.

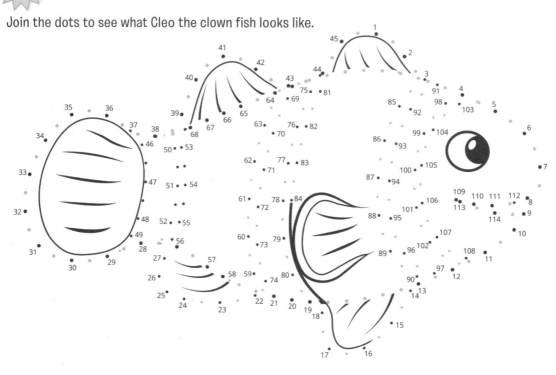

234 Momo's shadow

Momo the monkey can't find her real shadow! Can you help find it?

235 Your favourite things

Doodle your favourite things on your pack of cards!

Materials required: Twelve 2.5x3.5" rectangular card papers, pencil, eraser, sketch pens or paint

Method:
1. Pick 12 of your favourite things to do or eat.
2. Draw each of them one by one, on the back of your cards.
3. Once you are done, shuffle them and play a game with your friends or family.

236 The quarter dart

This is a tricky dart board. Can you guess what the missing number is that replaces the question mark?

237 Food fiesta ↓↓↓

So much to eat, so little time! Try and find the delicious food items on the right within the image on the left.

238 Wacky words! ↓↓↓

From the pictures below, guess what the words are.

M1LLION _____

STOOD
MISS _____

PAwalkRK _____

S
T
A me
N
D _____

WALKING
ICE _____

239 Halloween fun

It's Halloween time in the city of Greensville. Take a walk around using the path marked 1 to reach the other side marked 2. Remember, you can't jump over blocks.

240 Happy monsters

Get your pencils and paints out! It's time to draw and colour the images of the three cute monsters below.

241 Check this out!

Look at the image below for a few minutes. What do you see?

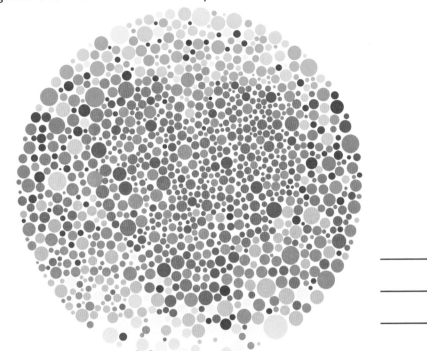

_____

_____

_____

242 Guess the floor

Read the paragraph below and figure out who gets off on which floor.

Six people go into a shopping mall and take the lift up from the underground parking lot. The shopping mall has six floors and each person has to go to a different floor. The lift stops at all the floors and someone gets out.

Lee rides for the longest time of the six. Mia gets off before Dave, but after Macy. Paul gets out before anyone else. Christy gets off before Macy, who gets out at the third floor. Who gets off at which floor? Tell us!

_____

_____

_____

_____

_____

243 Your pet

Turn your pet into a jigsaw puzzle!
Use the jigsaw pattern as your guide and draw an image of your pet on the page. Once that's done, make a copy of the image and paste it on a card paper. Ensure there are no air bubbles else it will end up becoming bumpy. When it dries up, take a pair of scissors and cut out according to the lines. Be sure to be neat while doing so. Mix up all the pieces and ask your family to put the pieces of the puzzle together to figure out what it is.

244 High above the ground

It's not a bird it's an origami airplane!
Bring out your supplies and let's make an airplane out of paper.

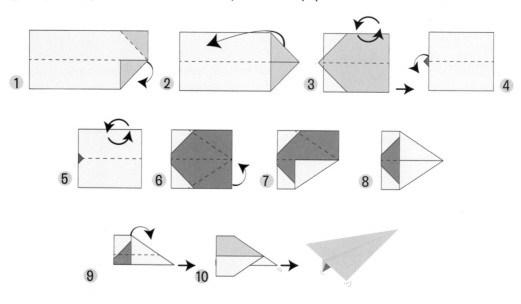

The universe and you

Draw yourself having a space adventure,
travelling through the universe.

246 Maximum display

Change one or more letters to make the next word.

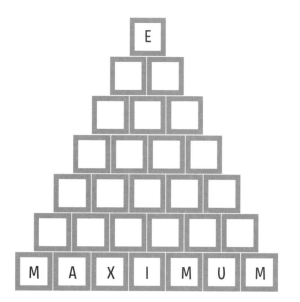

E

M A X I M U M

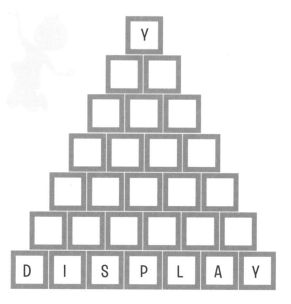

Y

D I S P L A Y

247 Animal name sudoku

Complete the grid so that every row, column and coloured box contains every letter from the word BEAR.

		B	
	E	A	
E	R		
A			

			B
	E		
		A	
R			

248 Uber cool helicopter

Make a helicopter tangram for fun.

Use the shapes to the right as your guide and cut them out on a square sheet. Once you're done, try assembling them together to form a helicopter. You can make a whole scrap book filled with these!

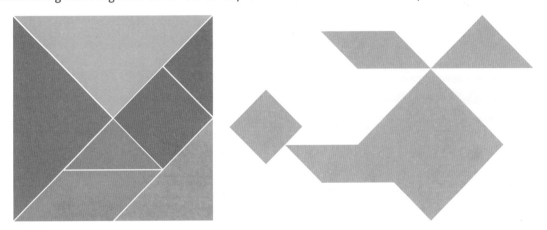

249 Know your manners

Let us see how well you know your manners.

Materials required: 10 rectangular card paper sheets of size 2.5 x 3.5 cms, sketch pens, glue, images representing manners

Method:
1. On one side of the card, ensure you paste images or draw representations of the different manners you need to know.
2. On the other side, write a line about what that kind of manner does.

250 Music instruments

Create doodles of 12 music instruments on the back of cardboard cards. Pick your instruments from the list below and copy the design on to the card paper.

Materials required: 12 2.5 x 3.5 inches rectangular card papers, pencil, eraser, sketch pens or paint

Method:
1. Use the smooth side of the card paper to make your designs.
2. First use pencil, then once you are sure of the design then colour it in with sketch pens or paints.

251 Sudoku stunner

Complete the grid so that every row, column and coloured box contains every digit from 1-9.

	2		7		1		8	
		1		9		6		
6		5		8		9		4
3								2
			1	3	6			
7								5
2		4		7		3		1
		7		1		2		
	6		5		2		7	

252 A cereal box

Imagine your favourite cereal company wants you to design the box it comes in.
What would you draw on it?

253 The hidden treasures

Pretend play to be a pirate for a day!

How to play: Get your parents to hide a few items like chunky imitation jewellery or rings, a telescope, a hat and everything a pirate would need to find hidden treasure. Ask your parents to give you a list of hidden items so you or/and your siblings have to look for around the house. If you find all of them within an allotted time, then your parents have to treat you. If you don't then you can do something for your parents like keep your room clean.

254 My imaginary car

Use your colours and draw an imaginary car, one that you really want to drive.
Give it a name too!

255 The crazy ferris wheel

Look at the picture below for a few minutes. Can you tell which way the Ferris wheel is moving?

256 At the library

Find words related to the library in the word search.

Book, science, literature, horror, fiction, categories, borrow, librarian, self help, mystery, murder, sci-fi

```
B B O O K S C I E N C E U N V
F F B Q O R T N J U T L H N S
P D O B A C O M E D Y K A N B
C U R S C Y H F M I Z I Y W J
X Q R U T A N O C N R S E H P
E Z O Y L I T E R A T U R E Q
A H W P T I J E R R J F Q C O
S R E T F Z V B G L O A Q B W
E Q S L C I I P D O H R Q A N
L Q R I P L C V J N R V L R I
F O X T M Y S T E R V I U N F
H W S X H E U Q I M H T E G I
E M S E L A N S R O E T E S C
L R P B H M L C K R N N B I S
P Z D M U R D E R R Q O J M W
```

257 Giddy words

How many words can you make in
5 minutes?
Remember, you need to use the
letter in the centre in every word
and there is at least one nine
letter word you will find.

Clue

Someone who
has lots of
energy

_____

_____

_____

_____

_____

_____

_____

258 Button games

Guess which button pattern comes next.

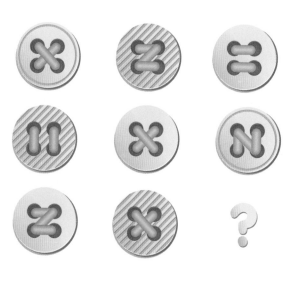

1

2

3

4

5

259 In the classroom

Find six hidden words in the image below.

260 Random doodle

Make your own masterpiece.

Get out your pens and pencils and draw whatever you like to draw. Once you're done drawing on the pattern below, get a photocopy of it and paste it on a card paper. When it dries up cut it out according to the pieces and then jumble them up. Ask your sibling to put it together!

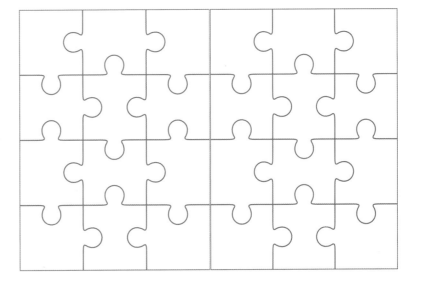

261 Galaxy slime

The colours of the galaxy are always fascinating. That's why today, it's time to make some galaxy inspired slime.

Materials required: six 120 ml glue bottles, three bowls (glass or plastic), water, food colouring, popsicle sticks for mixing, glitter, borax

Method:
1. In each bowl, pour out the contents of two 120 ml glue bottles.
2. Add 100 ml of water into each bowl and stir with the popsicle sticks.
3. Add blue food colouring into one bowl, purple in the second and pink in the last bowl. Stir again and then mix in the glitter while stirring continuously for a few minutes.
4. Once that settles, in a measuring bowl/cup add in a teaspoon of borax powder and pour 500 ml of warm water into it.
5. When the borax has dissolved, let the water cool.
6. Add about 3-5 tablespoons of the borax water mixture into the first bowl. Mix continuously and when your liquid substance becomes gooey and paste-like, your galaxy slime is ready!

262 Penguin march

Find the shadow that matches each penguin!

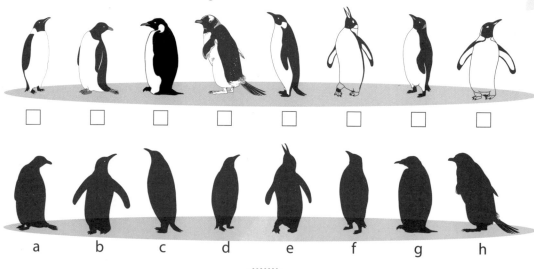

a   b   c   d   e   f   g   h

263 Add or delete ⫶⫶⫶

Look at the number below and see how you can make the highest number possible by moving just two matchsticks.

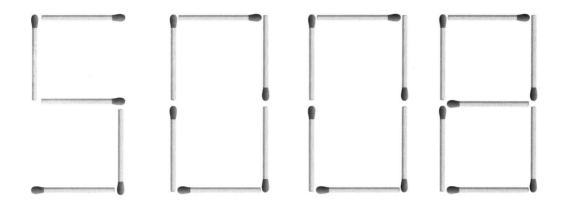

264 Little hearts ⫶⫶⫶

Can you find two identical hearts?

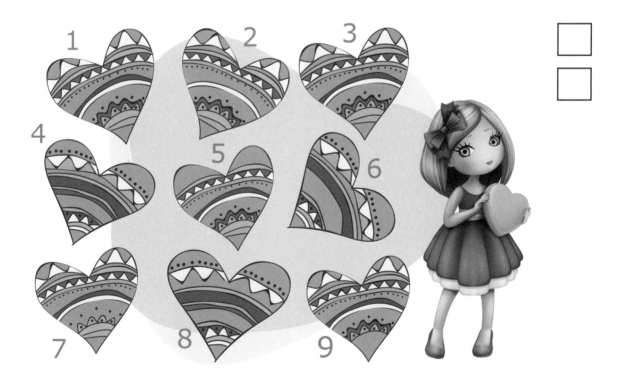

265 Magic squares

Every horizontal and vertical row adds up to 250. Fill the empty boxes with the right number to ensure that the numbers total 250!

145	30		40
70	45		10
18	95		72

266 Outdoor painting

Sue loves painting and finds her inspiration outdoors. It's your turn to complete the picture and colour it too. Draw what you think she has been inspired by.

267 The friendship ladder

Add, remove or replace a letter or more to move up the ladder and form the word 'Pal'.

Pal
	Hint: Rhymes with Dad
	Hint: A cheesy something
	Hint: Cast off
	Hint: On a bike or scooter
	Hint: She is all dressed in white
	Hint: An egg that is sunny side up
Friend

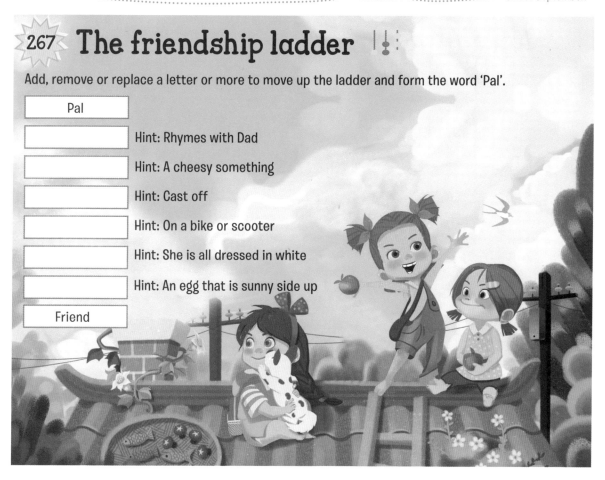

268 Catch 22

Can you guess the final sum in the puzzle below.

2	+	2	+	4	=	
+		+		+		+
5	+	1	+	1	=	
+		+		+		+
1	+	2	+	2	=	
=		=		=		=
	+		+		=	

269 A hot air balloon ride

Draw your own private hot air balloon that you can take wherever you go!

270 Noah's ark

Do you know the story of Noah's Ark? If not, ask your parents to tell you the story.
But for now, here's a list of words from the ark for you to find.

Instruction, Creatures, Preserve, Warning, Animals, Refuge,
Family, Timber, Night, Build, Right, Lived, Loyal, Flood, Save,
Door, Rain, Boat, Noah, Days, God, Ark

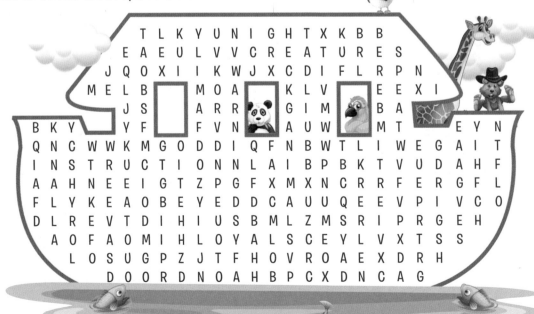

271 A little bit of me ⬇⬇⬇

Guess the answers to the questions below!

To complete a family dinner at your house, something is needed. Read the clue and guess what is missing. The answer can be found in time, meal, home and omelette; but not in snack, dessert, soup or vegetables.

_____

272 Tricky trek ⬇⬇⬇

Plan a scavenger hunt during a trek over a weekend.

How to play: Plan this with your school friends. Get your teacher to give you a list of things you can find during a trek. Write down the things you've found and compare it with the list she has given you. If you have got all, ask her to let you and your team lead the group walking back to campsite.

273 The mighty microscope !!!

Most of you may have seen this lab instrument.
Can you figure out how this microscope was
made using two tangram squares?

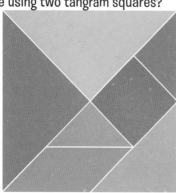

274 Chocolate balls with sprinkles !!!

Here's a recipe for an easy dessert you can make for your family!

Materials required: A pack of biscuits, cocoa powder, a can of condensed milk, sprinkles, butter

Method:
1. Crush a full packet of biscuits using a grinder, or by putting the biscuits into a plastic bag and crushing it with a rolling pin.
2. Add one tablespoon of cocoa powder. Slowly, add in the condensed milk and mix well until fairly smooth.
3. Grease your palms with butter. Take some of the chocolatey dough and roll it till it becomes a ball. Do this for the entire batch of dough.
4. Dip the balls into the sprinkles and let them chill in the freezer for 20 minutes. Yum!

275 Nocturnal animals

Nocturnal animals are those that stay up through the night and sleep during the day. Fill in the crossword to meet some of them using the clues below.

Optimistic **OCTOBER!**

Across

1. H_rm_tcr_b
2. B_shr_ts
3. D_ng_s
4. Hy_n_s
5. K_l_s
6. L__p_rd
7. T_g_rs

Down

1. A_rdv_rk
2. B_dg_r
3. B_t
4. Be_v_rs
6. Cr_ck_ts
7. H_mst_r
8. L__n
9. M__s_
10. P_ss_m
11. Sk_nk

167

276 Decorate a cake

Birthdays, special occasions, or just because you like it... cake is delicious.
Draw and decorate your very own cake using your favourite colours!

277 Matchstick muddle

Solve this puzzle by taking away six matchsticks to make TEN.

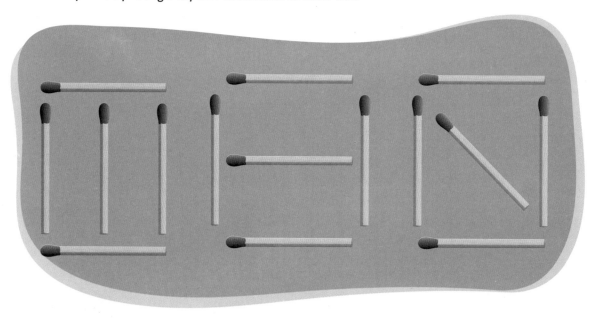

278 Nesting dolls

Find the matching pair within these nesting dolls.

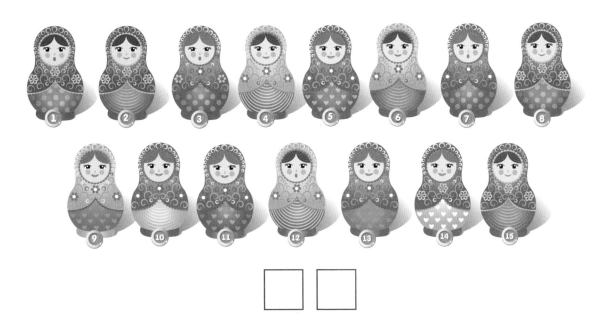

[ ] [ ]

279 The case files

Another missing number puzzle, another case to solve! Come on, use your magic math skills to solve this one!

		4	3	2		
	5	3	5	1	1	
6	1	2		3	3	1
	7	2	8	4	3	
		9	6	3		

280 Captain Mimi and the lost treasure ⅼⅼⅼ

Captain Mimi found some lost treasure on an island. Can you find all the differences from her expedition in the image below?

281 Mood swings ⅼⅼⅼ

Add, remove or replace one letter or more to move up the ladder.

Hint: Opposite of bad

Hint: Little Red Riding ____?

Hint: Simple past tense of shall

Hint: Can and _____

Hint: Opposite of wouldn't

Hint: From trees we get _____

Mood

282 Trying triangles

Guess how many triangles are there in the image below.

283 Fun weekend activities

Jodie and Alice have had an amazing weekend filled with lots of fun activities.
Can you unjumble the words below to figure out what they were doing?

1. Miswimgn

2. Utiagr

3. Acheb

4. Ripotdar

5. Ncicpi

6. Tarew gnikmod

284 Hurrah for halloween

This Halloween theme puzzle is just waiting to be solved! Look at the clues below and guess the answers.

Across

1. Kids threaten with these two things on Halloween
2. A witch sits on this to fly
3. _____ O Lantern
4. Kids often complain these are under their beds
5. The place where the dead rest

Down

1. Thirsty for blood and has an aversion to garlic
2. The father of vampires
3. Our body is made up of bones called a_____
4. Casper was a friendly what?
5. Halloween is famous for wearing scary _____
6. To scare
7. The Adam's family are _____ and spooky
8. Man turns into this when the moon comes out

285 Across the river

A man has to get a chicken, a fox and a sack of corn across a river. His boat can only carry him and one other thing.

If he takes the corn first, the fox will eat the chicken.
If he takes the fox first, the chicken will eat the corn.
So what does he do?

Write you answer here:

_____

_____

_____

_____

286 Tick the next pattern

Look carefully at the patterns below. Can you tell which ones come next?

287 Types of galaxies

Time to bring out the space nerd in you with these galaxy themed flash cards.
Materials required: 10 rectangular card paper sheets of size 2.5 x 3.5 cms, sketch pens, glue, images representing the different types of galaxies

Method: Find images of the 10 different types of galaxies using the list below.

1. Milky Way
2. LMC
3. Andromeda
4. Cigar
5. Pinwheel
6. Sombrero
7. Whirlpool
8. NGC
9. Tadpole
10. Hoag's Object

Once you've found the images, cut and paste them on one side of the card paper.
On the other side, write a line or two or even just the name of the galaxies. Once dried and done, shuffle the cards and ask your friends or siblings to help you play.

288 A fairy tale life

Find the words related to a fairy tale and circle them!

witch, giant, stepsister, castle, stepmother, prince, princess, dragons, ogre, powers, haunted, fairies, wand, banshee, magic, wail, midnight

```
G I A N T T B Y X R Z P N G C
P O W E R S B J W Z Z I F Z C
S T E P S I S T E R W R H E A
M S W M F F G P O T I A N S S
K T R Q O N J H I K Q M N F T
B P E E H S N A B V D A P D L
D R A G O N S Q C F W G E S E
J J V V D C D T D A V I H M F
P R I N C E S S E I A C C L L
N Q P R I N C E T R I E E B N
T R Z Q J K F K N I S A S N W
D W I T C H H Z U E Z G W O Z
G I O I U Y E U A S L P G G J
R S T E P M O T H E R T Q R Z
P S L Y B B G Q F O V C Z E D
```

289 Monkey see, monkey do

Help the monkey get through this maze below to reach the bananas.

 START

FINISH

290 Newspaper photo frame decorations

Bring out a bunch of old newspapers! It's time to make lovely decorations with them.

Materials required: Newspaper, glue, paints, scissors, old photo frame, pencil

Method:
1. Cut strips of newspaper and keep them aside.
2. Take one strip at a time, brush on some glue and start rolling it up against the pencil. Slide each one off the pencil and leave it to dry.
3. Make only as many as you want, so that you can spend more time painting them. Once you have your rolls ready, get the photo frame out and decide how you want to decorate it.
4. Once the rolls are dry, paint them with bright colours.
5. Stick them on to your frame and leave it to dry overnight.

In the morning, your lovely photo frame will be ready for use!

291 Sand bucket ⌄⌄⌄

Complete the image by creating a beach scene and solving the maze on the bucket.

292 Something fishy ⌄⌄⌄

Out of the water they cannot breathe. Under the water, they happily live.
Bring a piece of paper and together let's make a fish out of water!

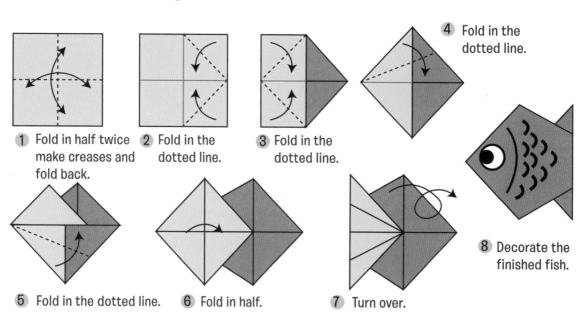

4 Fold in the dotted line.

1 Fold in half twice make creases and fold back.

2 Fold in the dotted line.

3 Fold in the dotted line.

5 Fold in the dotted line.

6 Fold in half.

7 Turn over.

8 Decorate the finished fish.

293 Draw your favourite villian

Whether from a movie or a cartoon, draw your favourite villian character here!

294 Laughter is the best medicine

Can you tell what these clues describe?

+ ✔ + les = _____

+ + = _____

295 Cycle all the way

Turn your cycling obsession into an indoor activity by making yourself a paper cycle tangram by using two square sheets.

296 Missing number

What's the missing number? Figure out the logic.

297 Papercut lampshades

Make a pretty paper lampshade with a little help from an adult!

Materials required: Craft paper, scissors, paper knife, pencil, ruler, tape

Method:
1. Choose two contrasting colours of craft paper for this activity.
2. Cover one sheet of craft paper by drawing triangles of different sizes, making sure that they don't overlap or touch each other.
3. Now cut out all the triangles from the paper. You will be left with a lattice.
4. Repeat this with the rest of the paper.
5. Once you are done, place one sheet of paper on top of the other. Fold them together into a single cone and tape it closed.
6. Put a bulb through the cone and plug it in.

298 Everyday words

Find the words that you use very often while speaking.

```
I C L S Q P A R K I N G L O T W P
B U G N B U I L D I N G A Q U W M
C L F O F U L A T A X I I D N A H
I T A I Q L I P C I T Y R E I T H
U U C S J B G A E X U L P P V E B
D R T E O U H R X S E I O A E R U
X E O P B S T T C K F B L R R P S
H S R O S I S M I Y T R L T S O Y
G P Y L S N P E T S H A U M I L P
A P X L U E U N E C E R T E T L E
R V V U B S B T M R A Y I N Y U O
B D Z T W S A E E A T P O T Y T P
A A H I A Z N J N P E W N S P I L
G K J O V N K K T E R X B T G O E
E O C N R O A D M R N R D O F N A
P R U D E P E O P L E C A R S X O
M A N Y P E O P L E Y Z L E I W N
```

Air pollution	Jobs
Apartment	Library
Bank	Lights
Building	Many people
Business	Noise pollution
Busy people	Parking lot
Cars	Road
City	Rude people
Cultures	Skyscraper
Department	Subway
Store	Taxi
Excitement	Theater
Factory	University
Garbage	Water pollution

299 Turn on the lights!

Join the bulb to the switch that lights it up.

300 Carrot flute

It's time to turn a boring vegetable like a carrot into a bright fun music instrument like a flute. You will need your parents help while doing this.

Materials required: Cutting board, a knife, 1 carrot (raw and thick), a thin scooper or butter knife, twist drill bit

Method:
1. On a cutting board, hold a carrot up from its root.
2. Chop the thick end off.
3. Use a scooper or a butter knife to scrape out the filling enough to make it hollow.
4. Once that's done, chop another ½ inch of the carrot to make a minor opening. Cut diagonally.
5. Take the thick part of the carrot and make a circular stopper by slitting it diagonally. However, make sure you don't cut through the entire carrot.
6. Put the stopper in to block the opening just enough to blow through it.
7. Add four small holes using a twist drill bit and your flute is ready.

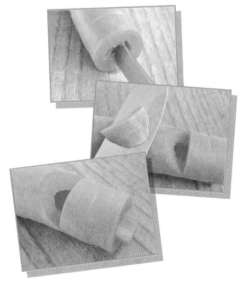

301 Tree huggers

Turn this lifeless tree into a pretty and luscious green one by painting on leaves, colourful flowers and birds!

302 Alan and his father

Can you guess Alan's father's age?

Alan is 45 years old, while his dad is 73. Calculate how many years ago Alan was one-third the age of his father.

_____

_____

_____

_____

_____

303 Ballerina prima donna

Find up to eight differences between the two ballerina images.

304 Balloon drum

Make your own cool handmade drum set.

Materials required: One tin can (preferred, else a big toilet paper roll), three balloons, three elastic bands, one pencil or plastic drum sticks

Method: For tin can:
1. Ensure that the lid is off.
2. Cut the narrow part of the balloon and use the wide part to cover the opening of the tin can.
3. Secure the balloon skin with an elastic band.
4. Use the pencil or plastic drum stick to beat the make-shift drum!

For the toilet paper roll:
1. Make sure both end of the roll are open
2. Either use a pretty wrapping paper to decorate the roll with or stick a white sheet of paper. You can later draw/paint on it after you've stuck it.
3. Cut the narrow parts of two balloons. Stretch them over the opening of the rolls and secure with elastic bands on both sides.
4. Once you've painted it, then use the plastic drum sticks to play it.

Pixie the missing fairy

Bring out your colour pencils and turn this scene into a pretty one!

306 Mind the gap

Can you guess the missing number in the gap? Use addition or subtraction to figure out what the last number is.

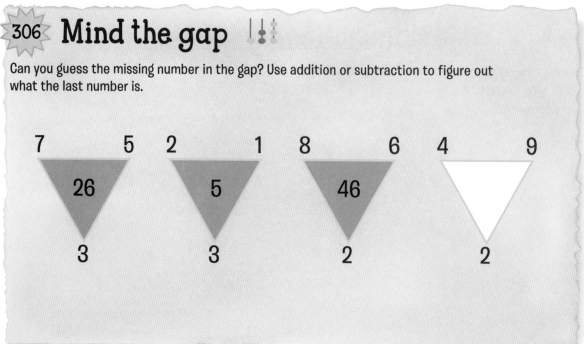

307 Trippy butterfly

Are the butterfly wings moving? Stare at them for a minute and see.

308 Day at the mall

Find at least eight differences between the pictures given below.

309 An everlasting smile

Add, replace or remove one letter or more to go to the next word.

	Hint: A ____ of pizza
	Hint: What is a small island called?
	Hint: The floor is decorated with marble ____
	Hint: 3.2 kilometres makes two ____?
Smile	
	Hint: Opposite of worst
	Hint: When you are tired, you need to take some ____
	Hint: The highest mountain in India is called Mount ____?
	Hint: Drop the 'ing' from everlasting
Everlasting	

310 Brave soldier

Change, add or remove letters to make the next word in the pyramid.

311 Back to the circus

Help Mr Clown get back to the circus using the correct lane.

312 Pencil shaving's art

Creativity can be inspired from anywhere, even pencil shavings! So let's use them to create a beautiful butterfly.

Materials required: Pencil shavings, canvas paper, colour pencils, glue

Method:
1. On a piece of canvas paper, lightly draw the outline of a butterfly.
2. Take yellow, red, green or brown pencil shavings and start sticking them on the outline.
3. Use a variety of coloured shavings to make your butterfly beautiful.
4. To be more creative you can draw a background scene to your art work. For example, use your paints and crayons to colour plants and flowers and create an amazing garden scene.

313 The dancing couple

Add musicians, guests and a chandelier hanging from the ceiling to complete this image.

314 Figure this out

What is the missing number?

If 817 = 7,
909 = 9,
453 = 3,
then, what is 1246 = ?

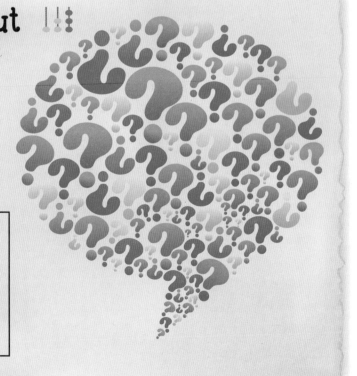

315 Wake up your brain

Think and answer the following question.

I am an ODD number.
Take away an alphabet and I become EVEN.
What number am I ?

_____

316 My menu

If you were a chef, what would you cook in your restaurant? Doodle a makeshift menu for your customers.

317 African animals

Find the list of African animals and birds in the puzzle below.

```
D K O B G N I R P S H R R C H
Z E E O P E L E P H A N T O O
T E L G A E L A I T R A M B S
O N I N N Z U I Z G T L H R T
M O D I G N U D F E E L V A R
L O O M O A C K U V B I K E I
E B C A L P Z H O K E R D F C
O A O L I M L E E B E O A F H
P B R F N I V S L E S G J A Y
A I C W O H L Q M L T M M R E
R H I N O C E R O S E A E I N
D S U M A T O P O P P I H G A
```

Baboon	Hartebeest
Cheetah	Hippopotamus
Chimpanzee	Hyena
Cobra	Kudu
Crocodile	Leopard
Elephant	Lion
Flamingo	Martial eagle
Gazelle	Ostrich
Gemsbok	Pangolin
Giraffe	Rhinoceros
Gnu	Springbok
Gorilla	Zebra

318 Cherry blossoms

Make your own Cherry Blossom shadow painting.

Materials required: A leafless branch, table lamp, pencil, eraser, paints

Method:
1. Use the light from a table lamp to cast a shadow over the page.
2. Get somebody to hold the branch over the page to form the shadow.
3. Draw an outline of the shadow using a pencil in the given empty space.
4. Once done, remove the branch and continue painting the shadow black or grey.
5. Add flowers on your branch painting by using white and pink colours.

319 Run chicks, run! 🎻

Nash, the naughty little fox is always trying to catch the chicks. Help them run to their mother before he eats them up!

320 Picnic basket 🎻

Everyone loves a picnic. What are the different foods you could pack into your picnic basket?

Across:
1. Muffins with icing
2. The meal between lunch and dinner
3. A fizzy drink
4. A sweet biscuit

Down:
1. The cooler version of tea
2. Layers of vegetables and cheese are used to make this
3. Crispy potato wafers

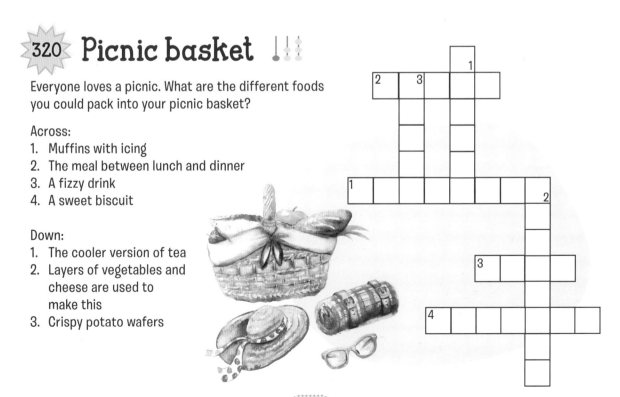

321 Party at the pizza parlour ↓↓↓

It's a night out at the pizzeria! Look at the image below and find the hidden words.

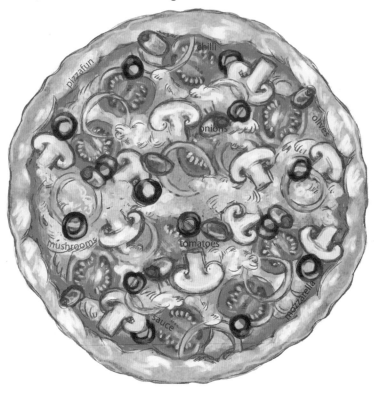

322 Hiking in the forest ↓↓↓

Can you find 10 differences between the two pictures?

323 ## Biscuit man

A biscuit man sells 1 biscuit pack for $1.
You can exchange 3 wrappers for 1 biscuit pack.
If you have $15, how many biscuit packs can you get?

 324 ## Piece the puzzle together

Can you tell which puzzle pieces fit into the spaces?

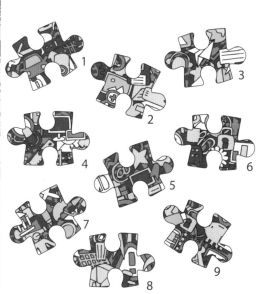

325 Match the profession !!!

In the image below, match the professionals with the jobs that they do.

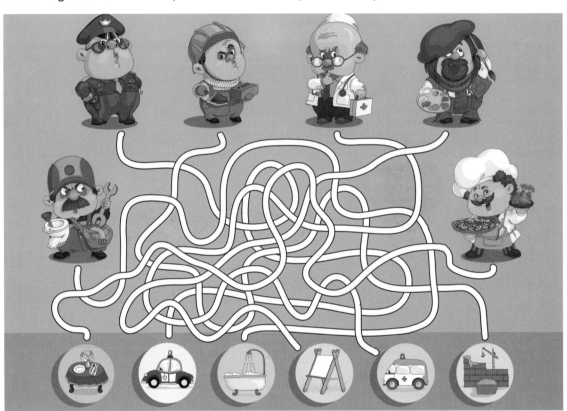

326 Matter of the chain !!!

A 10-foot long chain is nailed to the wall. It drops down 5 feet at the centre, from either end of that is nailed to the wall. Can you tell how far apart the two ends are from each other?

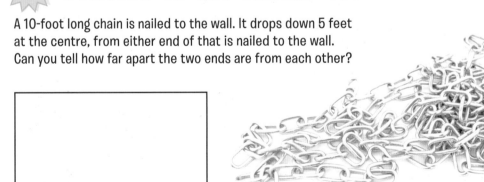

327 The final sum

What number will fill the space where the question mark is?

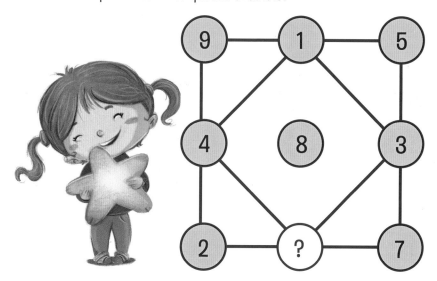

328 Magical christmas tree

How cool would it be to grow your own mini Christmas tree within minutes? Let's see how.

Materials required: blotting paper sheets, a mug, scissors, pen, a ladle, water, salt, household ammonia, liquid detergent, flat glass plate and food colouring

Method:
1. Pour 6 tablespoons of water in a mug. Then, add 6 tablespoons of liquid detergent to it followed by 1 tablespoon of household ammonia. Keep stirring in all the ingredients. Last, add in the 6 tablespoons of table salt into the mixture and stir until it is dissolved.
2. Now that your liquid is ready, start preparing the Christmas tree. Draw the outlines of two Christmas trees on two sheets of blotting paper.
3. Cut it out using a pair of scissors. Ensure you make a slit on both sheets, one on top and the other towards the middle bottom.
4. Slide the sheet with the slit on top over the other and place the tree on a flat glass plate or surface.
5. Dab some food colouring onto the edges of the tree and then pour the mixture over it. Wait a few minutes before the magic is revealed to you and soon you will have your own magical Christmas tree.

329 Reindeer mania

It's Christmas time and the elves have played a prank on Santa. You need to help him figure out which shadow belongs to which reindeer.

330 Diamonds are forever

How many triangles and quadrangles have been used there in this image?

331 Race to the house ⬇⬇⬇

After a walk in the fields, the Rupert family decided to race back home. Who got home first?

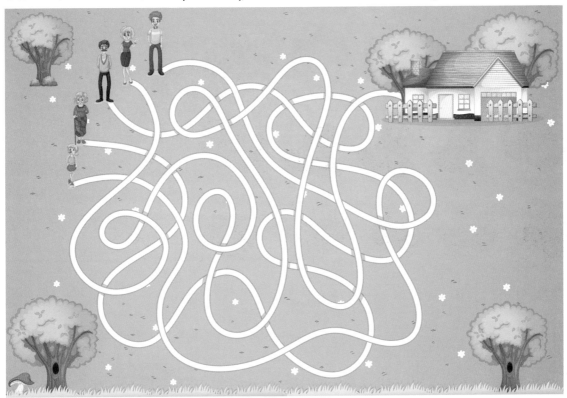

332 Christmas hunt ⬇⬇⬇

Celebrate the spirit of Christmas by asking your parents to hide five Christmas tree ornaments around the house.

How to play: Get your parents to make a list of ornaments they've hidden around the house. You and your friends need to team up and look for the items. Keep a bag or basket with you to carry back the ornaments. As and when you find an ornament, colour in the outlines in the picture. The first team who finds all the ornaments should be allowed to decorate the tree first or at least be given a gift!

333 Thanksgiving fiesta ⋮⋮⋮

Can you tell what comes next?

_____

_____

_____

334 Know your veggies ⋮⋮⋮

Use the list to find the vegetables in the word search.

```
E G G P L A N T C T E Z R B F
B A J Z R C K A H C E E A R R
C G N W G E R P U U W E S A E
O Z A J W R B T A O Y E B B P
L B E R O A T M L R O W J U P
L R G T L E T F U T S Z Y H E
A O A R L I I E A C U N F R P
R C B U Z L C T R D U K I W E
D C B T U L O W R C M C K P R
M O A A F P A S P A R A G U S
E L C B S W T V E Y D E C R L
L I Z A E O D R A H C I S H O
O C E G D A N O I N O V S S D
N P Q A P H N T Y X I S V H Q
I B A R L H O K N P I N R U T
```

Asparagus	Lettuce
Bean	Melon
Beet	Onion
Broccoli	Parsnips
Cabbage	Peas
Carrot	Pepper
Cauliflower	Potatoes
Chard	Radish
Collard	Rhubarb
Cucumber	Rutabaga
Eggplant	Turnip
Garlic	Watercress
Kohlrabi	

335 Toy truck planters

Do you have a toy truck or a car that is lying around collecting dust? Bring it out, because you are going to become a mini gardener. Here's how you make a toy planter.

Materials required: An open top toy truck or car, potting soil, gravel, bits of charcoal, stone crops of your choice

Method:
1. Clean out your toy truck and ensure that the four sides are closed off. Get an adult to help with this.
2. Add the gravel as your bottom layer. Cover it with a few bits of charcoal.
3. Add a thick layer of potting soil (not sand) and then add the stone crop.
4. Spray/sprinkle some water on it and place it in your garden or on your windowsill.

336 Wonderland

Can you solve this puzzle and figure out the clothes worn in winter?

Across
1. A shirt with a high neck collar
2. You tie this around your neck to keep warm
3. Another word for vacations
4. Ankle-length shoes
5. A thicker blanket
6. A jacket with a covering for the head

Down
1. The season during November to January
2. A pullover that keeps you warm
3. Feeling cold
4. A covering for the hands

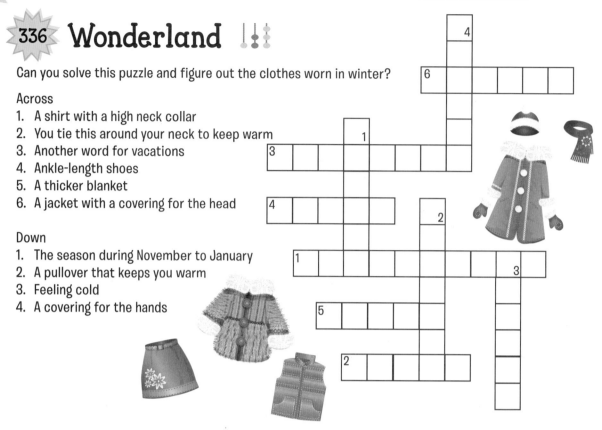

337 Tangram paper turtle

Take a cue from the ninja turtles and make yourself a paper tangram turtle for keeps. Use one square sheet and draw the shapes accordingly. Cut them out and figure out how to make the turtle.

338 Season's greetings

Change, add or delete one letter or more in the seasons greeting.

	Hint: Wish someone a Good Morning is to _____ them.
	Hint: To entertain someone with food or movie
	Hint: The act of withdrawing to a safe place
	Hint: When you betray a state you commit_____
	Hint: Another word for cause
Seasons	
	Hint: You must give the _____
	Hint: The present continuous tense of need
	Hint: _____ the dough makes the bread better
	Hint: The present continuous tense of read
	Hint: A conference with people
Greetings	

339 The cat who lost her bowl

Help Gul the cat find her way to the milk bowl.

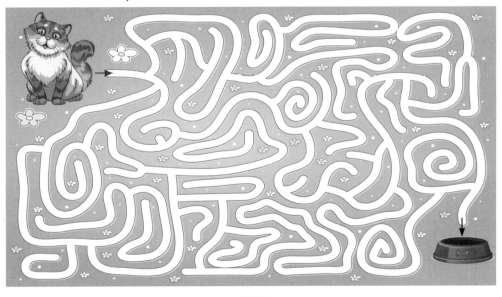

340 Cross number puzzle

Add or subtract the numbers to get your answers!

Across:
1. 73 - 28
3. 58 - 2
5. 112 + 749
7. 7,069 - 1,924
10. 2,781 + 1,477
12. 44 + 125
13. 4 + 78
14. 1,730 - 750
16. 313 + 209
17. 21 + 34
19. 21 + 616
21. 170 + 8,248
23. 7,089 - 2,944
25. 395 - 119
26. 6 + 5
27. 56 - 23

Down:
1. 345 + 4,503
2. 8,305 - 2,683
3. 2 + 53
4. 555 + 5,555
6. 7 + 8
8. 3 + 43
9. 62 - 3
11. 412 + 480
15. 491 + 337
16. 5,976 - 235
17. 2,472 + 2,701
18. 74 + 5,789
19. 86 - 22
20. 45 - 14
22. 3 + 39
24. 13 + 38

341 Out in the field

Match the missing pieces to complete the pretty image.

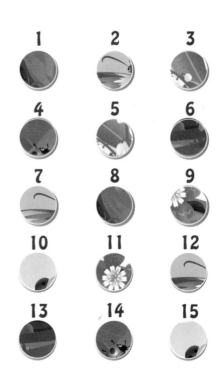

342 # Math tricks

Look at the boxes below and guess what number comes in place of the white box.

If

1	+	1	=	5
2	+	2	=	20
3	+	3	=	45
4	+	4	=	

 343 # My favourite teacher

Here's a picture of a classroom. Draw your favourite teacher at the blackboard teaching you your favourite subject.

344 Snowmen everywhere

Can you find your way back home among the many snowmen that surround the path?

345 # Piece of the heart

Use the shapes from the square box on the left to make a heart.

 346 # Ice skating

Winter is a good time to go ice skating. Draw a picture of a group of friends skating around the rink!

347 Carolling contest

Look at the clues and guess the names of the carols.

1. RUDE + ALL + F + +  + = _____

2. Jing L + =

   _____

3. V + + you + a + merry + Christmas =

   _____

4.  + the + halls + with + =

_____

348 Santa shares gifts

Can you spot the differences in the images of Santa distributing gifts below.

349 # Furniture in the house

Here's a fun zigzag word search for you. Try finding the different types of furniture in the puzzle. An example will make things easy for you.

B	E	D	H	B	E	D	I	S	D
C	O	U	C	O	A	R	D	F	R
A	F	O	S	C	B	U	F	U	E
W	A	R	D	H	T	E	F	T	S
E	B	O	R	A	I	T	N	O	S
B	M	I	R	V	R	A	B	R	E
O	R	O	R	A	N	I	L	C	D
O	S	T	E	S	Y	T	E	U	R
K	H	E	L	F	O	T	T	P	A
C	A	S	E	N	A	M	O	B	O

Bed, Dresser, Sofa, Bookcase, Futon, Table, Buffet, Mirror, Vanity set, Chair, Ottoman, Wardrobe, Couch, Shelf, Cupboard, Sideboard

 350 # Let's decorate with ribbons

Festive seasons are a perfect reason to decorate a house! Can you find two identical sets of ribbons?

351 Christmas holidays

Unjumble the letters to get the final word. Then, make as many words as you can from it.

LIHDOAYS

_____
_____
_____
_____
_____
_____

SHAMISTCR

_____
_____
_____
_____
_____

352 Walk in the wild

Create a jungle trail around the boy.

353 # The milkman puzzle

Guess the answer.

Marty, the milkman has two empty jugs - a three gallon one and a five gallon one. He needs to measure one gallon of milk without wasting any... Can he do it? If yes, explain how he can.

_____

_____

_____

_____

_____

 354 # Skater kids

Stop these kids from crashing their sleighs into one another.

355 Animal doodles ⬇⬇⬇

How many animals are there in this picture? Can you name them all?

356 Three dimensional image ⬇⬇⬇

Can you tell which way the image is moving? Gaze at the ball for a few minutes and see.

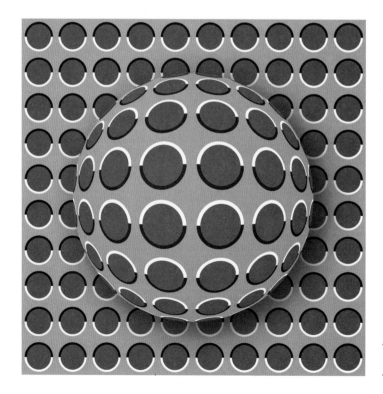

_____

_____

357 Bleeding tissue art

Let your creativity soar by making art using tissue paper. Go all out!

Materials required: Canvas paper, bleeding art tissue paper or colourful crepe paper, water in a spray bottle, paints

Method:
1. On the canvas paper, lay out bits of the tissue paper in any design you like.
2. Spray water over the tissue. When it is completely wet, put another sheet of canvas paper over it and press down firmly.
3. Keep it aside for a few minutes. Once it is dry, remove the top sheet of canvas paper and the tissue.
4. Your tissue paper art is ready!
5. Add doodles using white paint to make the painting prettier!

358 Find the mistake ⦙⦙⦙

Can you guess what's wrong with the the activity?

_____
_____

359 The pyramid of pizzeria ⦙⦙⦙

Replace, remove or add one letter or more to reach the top of the pyramid.

360 # Christmas spirit

Find the differences between the two pictures.

361 Festive puzzle

Look at the images and solve the puzzle.

Across		Down	
2.		1.	
6.		3.	
7.		4.	
10.		5.	
11.		8.	
12.		9.	

362 Reindeer face

Draw two funny faces under the antlers to make reindeers.

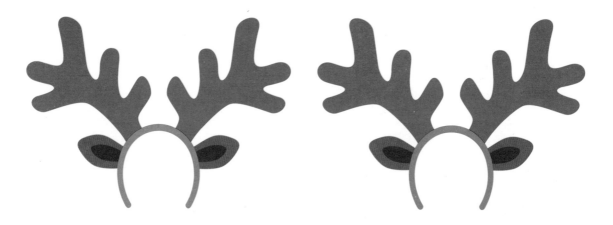

363 # Santa Claus is coming to town

Add a scene to this picture. Make it colourful and festive to celebrate Christmas!

364 # Oh so many Santas

Guess how many Santa's are there in the image below.

365 Best friends forever

Make your best friend a picture puzzle.
Draw a caricature of you and your best friend over the given pattern below and get it photo copied onto a card paper. Once you have that, cut along the line and then mix up the pieces. This can make for a fun birthday or friendship's day gift as well.

KNOW ANSWERS!

Activity 1

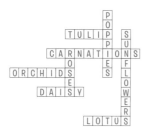

Activity 2

Activity 3

Activity 4

satellite, list, last, set, sail, salt, slit, slate, sat, east, least, lest, test, tilts, silt, stall, stale, ales, sale, tales, tells, sell, eels, steal, tease, seat, lets, see, sea, seal, ease

Activity 6

FRIS + =
Frisbee

 + + =
Badminton

Activity 8

Activity 9

Activity 10

Button kept eating from the same feed dish because Phyllis drank milk and Ryan ate the fish and never ate the oats.

Activity 11

Activity 13

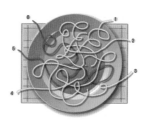

Activity 15

5 and 6 are joined

Activity 16

Activity 17

15 triangles and a pentagon

Activity 18

4 x 21 = 42 x 2 = 84
9 x 10 = 18 x 5 = 90
45 + 45 + 180 = 180 + 45 + 45 = 270
8 + 10 + 2016 = 1017 x 2 = 2034

Activity 19

Activity 20

Activity 21

Activity 22

Activity 23

When we look at optical illusions, our brain is trying to process the perception of information that is being gathered by the eye. The reason you feel this image is moving is due to the colour contrast and how the shapes are positioned.

Activity 24

Activity 26

Activity 27

Activity 31

33

Activity 32

Race
Trace
Grace
Lace
Mace
Ace
Pace
Space

Activity 33

One person was going to St. Ives.

Activity 34

Activity 35

Activity 37

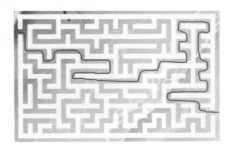

Activity 39

Activity 40

1. Crying over spilled milk
2. Piece of cake
3. Chip of the old block

Activity 41

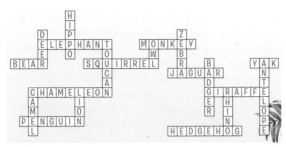

Activity 43

Cats and dogs

Activity 44

Courage, Brave, Strength

Activity 45

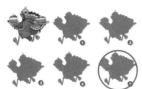

Activity 46

You'd have 3 apples.

Activity 47

There were only 3 of them, the grandfather, the father and his son.

Activity 48

Activity 52

Crisp
Lisp
List
Mist
Last
Past
Fast
Fist
Fish
Dish

Activity 53

Activity 54

7 # 7 # 77 # 7 # 7 = 497

7 + 7 x 77 - 7 x 7 = 497

Activity 55

Activity 56

Activity 58

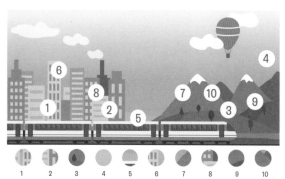

Activity 59

PANCAKES

Activity 60

Activity 62

An Arrow

Activity 63

1. 11:55
2. The seconds hand lies on:
The third letter, of this time, is also a math sign.
The second is an 'I', and the first is the number 7 on a keypad. 6:00
The hours hand lies on: The last day of the month of June. 6:30

Activity 64

Activity 66

8:45, if you left it at the same place.

21:50, if you leave it at the same place.

Activity 67

```
A X Y P F H J I C H B S
M L P R U F E U A P G T O U
A S T O R K F A Z P K J P E L
Z J T U Y U F L Q P T E Z K
E W M D O A U P K T S V F O Y
D E R J H P S G U E H O U I X
D C L C Z B V Y Z B J V L R I
L U C A E T K F E B C A H R P
R V W H T H O U G H T F U L A
V H A I O E A X B S O M Y A K
P N Q I V I D Z C I F U B C R
D C O N F I D E N T I T B R O
R Y Q O O S A M U S E D K A O
F Y L C B T N M F N J T Z T
D E L I G H T E D Y Y R B D T
```

Activity 69

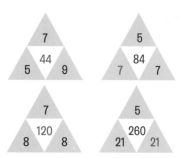

Activity 71

Activity 74

Drive
Driver
Diver
Dave
Dare
Harp
Sharp
Share
Scare
Scar
Car

Activity 75

	Dragon	Manatee	Sea Serpent	Unicorn
Sergei	●			
Darius				●
Mishka			●	
Ursla		●		

Activity 76

It is not possible for everyone to get their own rooms. Also, the second guest should have gone to the second room because guest number 13 was waiting in the first room.

Activity 79

Activity 80

Activity 81

Activity 82

The Letter E

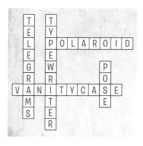

Q: What comes twice in a week, once in a year and never in a day?

Activity 83

Lighthouse
Captain
Submarine
Underwater

Activity 84

Activity 86

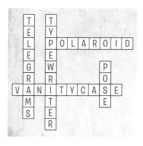

Activity 88

"If you want the children, answer this riddle!" Dr Evil.
9428 4637 ROUND AND 276863 ON A 467732225?
What goes round and around on a horseback?

A 22768735.
A Carousel

Activity 89

Water
Walker
Walk
Talk
Stalk
Chalk
Chalice
Malice
Alice
Ice

Activity 90

Activity 91

Activity 93

```
      E
V     P
O   I N N E R C O R E
L   N     N
C   N     E
M A N T L E     O
  N       C R   U
  O R B I T R   T
  T       U C   E
    E A R T H Q U A K E
            T S   C
                  O
                  R
                  E
```

Activity 94

Activity 95

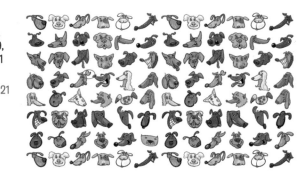

Activity 96

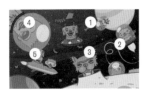

Activity 97

If
2 = 6,
3 = 13,
4 = 20,
5 = 30,
6 = 42
then
9 = 90

If
12 + 12 = 9,
25 + 25 = 9,
18 + 18 = 81
then
29 + 29 = 121

Activity 99

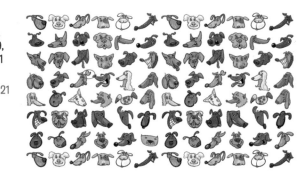

Activity 100

136	246
56 + 80	122 + 124
24, 32, 48	68, 54, 70
232	330
96 + 136	170 + 160
95, 75, 85	43, 53, 83
291	348
122 + 169	234 + 164
20, 102, 67	150, 84, 80

Activity 101

Win
Worn
Torn
Ton
Toll
Tall
Tale
Take
Tame
Team

Activity 102

Activity 103

Labrador, Pomeranian,
Irish Setter, Dalmation

Activity 104

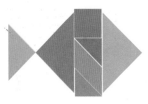

Activity 105

Activity 106

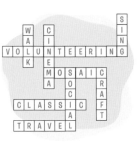

Activity 108

porridge, pride, ridge, ride, rider, pier, dire, red, drop, per, gore, pore, drier, ripe, grid, grip, ore, rig, gripe, gored, pored, pro

Activity 110

Eel
Peel
Meal
Teal
Seal
Sea

Activity 112

A	O
AN	ON
AND	TON
HAND	TONE
HANDY	STONE
SHANDY	HONEST

Activity 113

Activity 114

Yes. You can if you are able to push the coin and cork inside the bottle, you may be able to pull out the coin if the cork doesn't block the neck of the bottle.

Activity 117

Mrs B, your cover has been compromised. You need to leave town asap. Arrangements have been made.

Activity 120

The time is 8.10 am.

Activity 121

Activity 122

Activity 123

A to 2, B to 4, C to 1, D to 5 and E to 3.

Activity 124

When you look at the image carefully, there are pillars in white and the negative space created between the pillars are human figures.

Activity 125

Gallery
All
Mall
Tall
Talk
Tack
Pack
Park
Part
Art

Activity 126

Activity 127

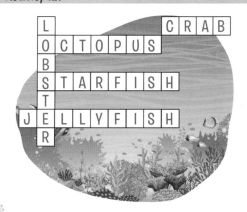

Activity 129

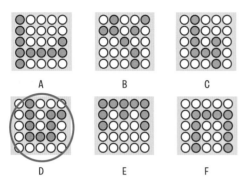

A   B   C

D   E   F

Activity 130

Activity 131

dreamcatcher, ache, arch, dream, cream, team, tame, rare, rear, tear, art, teacher, teach, heat, hate, heater, hater, act, dart, cart, heart, mart, meat, charm, harm, dare, hare, hear, mare, mar, rat, rate, date, drama, catch, cat, hat, dame, dam, ace, race, mace, mate

Activity 132

Activity 134

1	3	6	2	5	9	7	4	8
7	2	5	4	1	8	9	3	6
4	8	9	3	6	7	1	5	2
3	6	4	7	8	5	2	1	9
5	1	8	6	9	2	3	7	4
9	7	2	1	3	4	6	8	5
2	4	1	5	7	6	8	9	3
8	5	3	9	2	1	4	6	7
6	9	7	8	4	3	5	2	1

Activity 135

Crème De la Crème
Patisserie Specials
1. Chocolate
2. Croissants
3. Strawberry Truffle
4. Tiramisu
5. Choco pastry
6. Black Forest

Activity 137

Activity 138

10 monsters

Activity 139

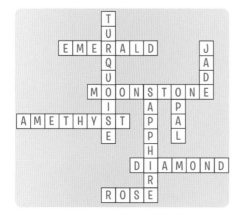

Activity 140

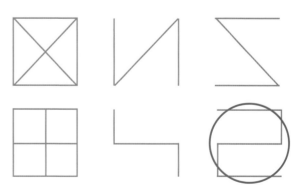

Activity 141

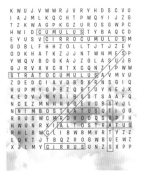

```
K W U J V W W R J V R Y H D S C V U
I A J M L K Q C H T P W Q Y I J Z G
T Z K W A G P K G Z U R O S G W P C
H W I D C U M U L U S T Y B A Q C D
E Y U S V C I R R O C U M U L U S M
G D B L F H H Z O L L T J T J Z E V
O D K H A T K Z J J N T W N M E S P
Y W Q V B O G K A J Z G L A S U J B
G J R V X V C R T X C Q N Z T P W W
S T R A T O C U M U L U S A V M V U
Z D E D C I A W H B S X R N S G I Q
H U P M V G P B Z Q R T U Y N E J X
K E D V J N Y S I B S S T S A A F Q
N C E Z M N H H V O E V O B S V J L
N I M B O S T R A T U S Q T I O U
R R U S W C M R D R O D Q S R P F H
H W U N R X I A L T O S T R A T U S
R H L B W C L I B W B M V R T Y Z Z
E Q K T J T B Q Z R O G W B U E W Z
X J L M Y C I R R U S U N Z S X P P
```

Activity 143

Activity 144

2	+	1	+	6	=	9
+		+		+		
7	+	3	+	8	=	18
+		+		+		
9	+	5	+	4	=	18
=		=		=		
18		9		18		

Activity 145

Sky
Sly
Fly
Flow
Flea
Flee
Glee
Glue
Clue
Blue

Activity 147

Activity 148

4 5 7 2 5

Activity 150

flask, red, compass, bucket, lantern, back pack, gum boots, map, fishing lures, fish coral, binoculars, chair, knife, hat

Activity 151

```
G D I D B D T E I G C O C O O N Y W
C F P E V R V T A Y B Q I B C T X F
O Z F I R E F L Y N R C V W M U L B
D R A G O N F L Y P L S Q Y W B E E
P J A T E R M I T E A C C N A N T E
G Z M S X A V G Q T S I A T L E T T
S L O Z H C F C S I P D R R E F E L
I G S U V G L E O S I K D T I F P E
X J Q B E E J I R L N R U Y B Y F K
B P I C R I C K E T M A V O J P Q X
U U T K X F L E A M A C H O G B L Y
P N O A T J U G K A N H P E R Y N M
T H G L O W A N T P I E Z D Q O H O
O N W A A D G N D H S S P I B B F H
T G H G R A S S H O P P E R F N T L
```

Activity 152

1. Big bad wolf
2. Tree cut into half
3. Trip around the world
4. Scrambled eggs
5. Somewhere over the rainbow
6. Quarterback

Activity 154

81, 90, 99, 108, 117, 126, 135, 144, 153, 162, 171, 180, 189, 198, 207, 216, 225.

Activity 155

Activity 157

2	7	8	5	6	4	3	9	1
4	9	1	7	3	2	6	8	5
6	5	3	1	9	8	4	2	7
5	1	2	8	4	3	9	7	6
3	4	7	6	5	9	8	1	2
9	8	6	2	7	1	5	3	4
1	2	9	4	8	6	7	5	3
8	6	5	3	2	7	1	4	9
7	3	4	9	1	5	2	6	8

Activity 159

Rocket,
spaceship,
alien,
satellite,
astronaut,
meteors,
stars,
launch

Activity 160

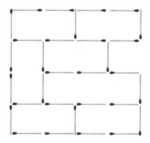

Activity 161

Activity 162

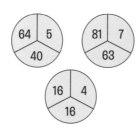

Activity 163

64	5
40	

81	7
63	

16	4
16	

Activity 165

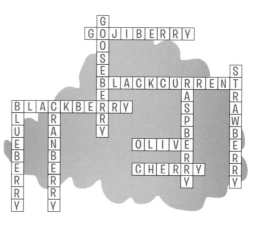

Activity 166

Activity 168

Season
Beaten
Eaten
Sweeten
Sweet
Sweat
Sweater

Activity 169

```
    B              B
   BO             BE
  BOO            BIN
 BOON           BING
ABOON          BLING
BALLON        BORING
BALLOON       SOARING
```

Activity 171

36 Squares

Activity 173

Activity 174

Robberies

Jewellery

Activity 175

Activity 176

Soda
Sod
Sad
Sid
Sit
Spit
Pit
Pet
Pep
Pop

Activity 178

Crossword:
FERRISWHEELS
POPCORN
CANDYFLOSS
RACE
ROLLERCOASTER
HOUSEOFMIRRORS
SLIDE
PERFORMANCES
TRAIN

Activity 179

21 Dogs

Activity 180

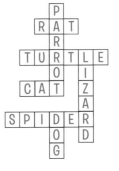

Crossword:
PARROT
RAT
TURTLE
LIZARD
CAT
SPIDER
DOG

Activity 182

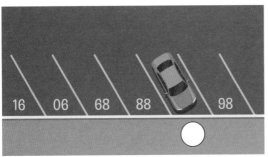

16   06   68   88   98

Answer: 87

Activity 183

Radio
Ratio
Rat
Hat
Heat
Seat
List
Sit
Visit
Vision
Television

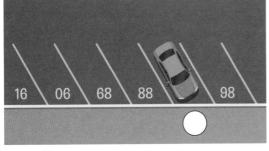

Activity 185

MICHEL
CAPTAINHOOK
TINKERBELL
WENDY
CROCODILE

Activity 186

Activity 187

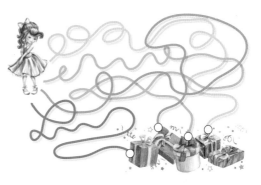

Activity 188

Word search grid with: BAGUETTE, BREAM, WAFFLE, BRUSCHETTA, BUTTER, ROLLS, CROISSANT, PANCAKES

Activity 189

Activity 190

IS
Logic: Assuming all alphabets equal twenty six numbers, the difference between the first is 2, 3 or 4 alternatively.
So, if E in WE = 5, G in SG = 7, that makes is 2 gaps. So the gap keeps increasing in the next pair. So finally you will come to IS which is 19, and four above the previous number.

Activity 192

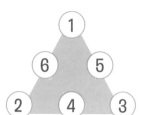

Activity 193

Activity 195

cosmopolitan, cosmo, pots, spot, sock, lion, loin, poling, ton, son, salt, lot, mon, stomp, pot, point, points, moon, toon, cot, cots, scot, moo, most, moist, lost, lots, omit, on, so, tons, stop, post, pistol

Activity 196

Trees, creepers, woods, sunrays, wild flowers, rocks and lake

Activity 197

Activity 198

Activity 199

"Today you are you, that is truer than true. There is no one alive who is youer than you" - Dr Seuss

Activity 201

Coyotes, rattle snakes, dingo, vulture, gecko and a scorpion

Activity 202

Activity 203

How do you make a 100 using four sevens and a one?
177 - 77 = 100

How do you make a 100 using 53 and Ali Baba's thieves?
60 + 40 = 100

Activity 204

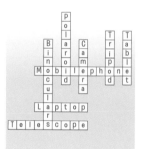

Activity 206

2	1	9	5	4	3	6	7	8
5	4	3	8	7	6	9	1	2
8	7	6	2	1	9	3	4	5
4	3	2	7	6	5	8	9	1
7	6	5	1	9	8	2	3	4
1	9	8	4	3	2	5	6	7
3	2	1	6	5	4	7	8	9
6	5	4	9	8	7	1	2	3
9	8	7	3	2	1	4	5	6

Activity 207

Activity 208

Spoon, Bread, Fork, Hats, Pie, Pumpkin, Turkey, Apples, Corncobs

Activity 209

Answer: Postman

Activity 210

```
              I
H        P       IN
 OH      PL      PEN
HOT      PAL     PLAN
HOST     PLAN    PLANS
HOSTS    PLATE   PLANTS
POSTAL   PLATES  PLATAIN
COASTAL  PLATEAU MOUNTAIN
```

Activity 214

Activity 215

Answer: One

Activity 216

Activity 217

Answer: FRUIT

Activity 219

Activity 220

Answer: 1386

Activity 221

Activity 223

How the clever burglar got away no one knows.
No clue was left behind. It was reported as a jewellery theft. No show of finger prints or footmarks.
The police looked through Mr and Mrs Morison's entire house. It was easy to steal anything from a rich old couple who stayed in a mansion. A witness reported.

Activity 225

Answer: 12

Activity 226

Activity 228

Chocolate

Strawberry

Caramel

Pineapple

Activity 229

Activity 232

Answer: 32

Activity 234

Activity 236

Answer: Zero

Activity 237

Activity 238

One in a million

Misunderstood

Walk in the park

Stand by me

Walking on thin ice

Activity 241

The illusion of a heart within the circle of colourful dots.

Activity 242

Level 1: Paul
Level 2 : Christy
Level 3: Macy
Level 4 : Mia
Level 5 : Dave
Level 6 : Lee

Activity 244

Activity 246

E	V
EX	YA
AXE	LAY
AXLE	LAYS
AXIOM	PLAYS
MAXIME	REPLAY
MAXIMUM	DISPLAY

Activity 247

A	E	B	R		A	R	E	B
R	B	E	A		B	E	R	A
E	R	A	B		E	B	A	R
B	A	R	E		R	A	B	E

Activity 248

Activity 251

4	2	9	7	6	1	5	8	3
8	3	1	4	9	5	6	2	7
6	7	5	2	8	3	9	1	4
3	1	8	9	5	7	4	6	2
5	4	2	1	3	6	7	9	8
7	9	6	8	2	4	1	3	5
2	8	4	6	7	9	3	5	1
9	5	7	3	1	8	2	4	6
1	6	3	5	4	2	8	7	9

Activity 256

Activity 257

Energetic, gent, net, rent, rite, ten, greet, teen, tier, er, get, tie, tiger, cite, nitre, green, rice

Activity 258

Answer:

1

Activity 259

Activity 262

Activity 263

Activity 264

Activity 265

145	30	35	40
70	45	125	10
17	80	25	128
18	95	65	72

Activity 267

Pal Bride
Pad Fried
Dip Friend
Rid
Ride

Activity 268

2	+	2	+	4	=	10
+		+		+		+
5	+	1	+	1	=	7
+		+		+		+
1	+	2	+	2	=	5
=		=		=		=
8	+	7	+	7	=	22

Activity 270

Activity 271

Answer: Me

Activity 273

Activity 275

Activity 277

Activity 278

Answer: 2 and 15

Activity 279

The middle number of each row is equal to half of the sum of the other numbers in the respective row.
So, sum of other numbers of middle row is
6+1+2+3+3+1=16
Half of 16 is 8.
So, answer is 8.

Activity 280

Activity 281

Good
Hood
Should
Could
Would
Wood
Mood

Activity 282

Answer: 25 Triangles

Activity 283

1. Miswimgn SWIMMING
2. Utiagr GUITAR
3. Acheb BEACH
4. Ripotdar ROADTRIP
5. Ncicpi PICNIC
6. Tarewgnikmod WATERKINGDOM

Activity 284

Activity 285

The man first takes the chicken, since the fox won't eat the corn and leaves it there.
Then he goes back for the corn, takes back the chicken otherwise it will eat up the corn.
He leaves the chicken behind and takes the fox to the other side where the corn is. Then he goes back for the chicken and takes all the three and moves on.

Activity 286

Activity 288

Activity 289

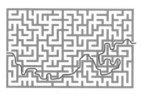

Activity 292

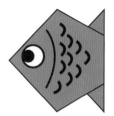

Activity 294

Rib tickles

Funny Bones

Activity 295

Activity 296

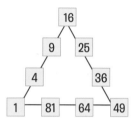

Activity 298

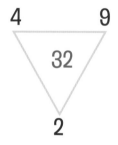

Activity 299

Activity 302

Alan was one-third of his father's age when he was 14. This goes back 31 years when his father was 42 years old.

Activity 303

Activity 306

4   9

32

2

Activity 308

Activity 309

Slice   Best
Isle   Rest
Tiles   Everest
Miles   Everlast
Smile   Everlastinh

Activity 310

B   D
BE   DO
BEE   OLD
BEAR   SOLD
BARE   SOLID
BRAVE   SOILDER

Activity 311

Activity 314

The answer is 4. Because
1+2+4+6=13 and 1+3 = 4.

Activity 315

Answer: 7
(SEVEN : Remove "S" = EVEN)

Activity 317

Activity 319

Activity 320

Activity 321

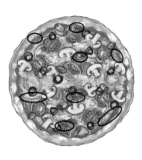

Activity 322

Activity 323

Answer: 20
($15 = 15 packs) +
(15 wrappers = 5 packs)

Activity 324

A = 4, B = 6, C = 9, D = 1,
E = 3, F = 7, G = 8, H = 5, I = 2

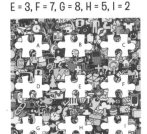

Activity 325

Activity 326

Both ends are nailed with
the same nail. In order for
the 10 foot chain to dip
down 5 feet it must dip 5
feet down and 5 feet up,
totalling up the length of
the chain.

Activity 327

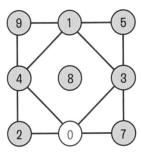

Activity 329

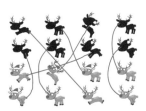

Activity 330

Answer: 73 triangles and
quadrangles

Activity 331

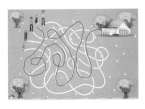

Activity 333

Activity 334

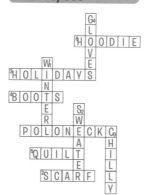

Activity 336

Activity 337

Activity 338

Greet   Needy
Treat   Needing
Retreat   Kneading
Treason   Reading
Reason   Meeting
Seasons   Greetings

Activity 339

Activity 340

Activity 341

Activity 342

If	1	+	1	=	5
	2	+	2	=	20
	3	+	3	=	45
	4	+	4	=	60

Activity 344

Activity 345

Activity 347

Rudolf the red nosed reindeer

Jingle Bells

We wish you a merry Christmas

Deck the halls with bows of holy

Activity 348

Activity 349

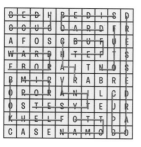

Activity 350

Activity 351

HOLIDAYS   CHRISTMAS

Holi   Mass
Days   Sat
Lid   Christ
Sad   Mast

234

Activity 353

The milkman filled the three gallon jug and then emptied the contents into the five gallon jug. He then filled the three gallon jug again and continued to fill the five gallon jug until it was full. The milk remaining in the three gallon jug was precisely one gallon.

Activity 354

Activity 355

Answer: 19 Animals

Activity 358

The is repeated twice in the instruction line.

Activity 359

Activity 360

Activity 361

Activity 364

Answer: 22 Santas

NO ANSWERS!

Below is the list of activities which do not have answers.

5, 7, 12, 14, 25, 28, 29, 30, 36, 38, 42, 49, 50, 51, 61, 65, 68, 70, 72, 73, 77, 78, 85, 87,92, 98, 107, 109, 111, 115, 116, 118, 119, 128, 133, 136, 142, 146, 149, 153, 156, 158, 164, 167, 170, 172, 177, 181, 184, 191, 194, 200, 205, 211, 212, 213, 218, 222, 224, 227, 230, 231, 233, 235, 239, 240, 243, 245, 249, 250, 252, 253, 254, 255, 260, 261, 266, 269, 272, 274, 290, 291, 293, 297, 300, 301, 304, 305, 307, 312, 313, 316, 318, 328, 332, 335, 343, 346, 352, 356, 357, 362, 363 and 365.

OTHER TITLES IN THIS SERIES

ISBN: 978-81-87107-58-3

ISBN: 978-81-87107-57-6

ISBN: 978-81-87107-56-9

ISBN: 978-81-87107-53-8

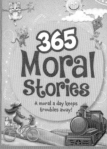

ISBN: 978-93-84225-31-5

ISBN: 978-93-81607-49-7

ISBN: 978-81-87107-55-2

ISBN: 978-81-87107-52-1

ISBN: 978-93-80069-35-7

ISBN: 978-93-80070-84-1

ISBN: 978-93-80070-83-4

ISBN: 978-93-80069-36-4

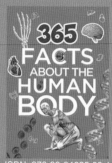

ISBN: 978-93-84625-93-1

ISBN: 978-93-83202-81-2

ISBN: 978-93-80070-79-7

ISBN: 978-93-84625-92-4

ISBN: 978-93-84225-33-9

ISBN: 978-93-84225-32-2

ISBN: 978-93-84225-34-6

ISBN: 978-81-87107-46-0